Non-Europhone Intellectuals

Non-Europhone Intellectuals

Ousmane Oumar Kane

Translated from French by Victoria Bawtree

CODESRIA

Council for the Development of Social Science Research in Africa
DAKAR

Originally published in French as *Intellectuels non europhones* by CODESRIA in 2003

© CODESRIA 2012
Council for the Development of Social Science Research in Africa
Avenue Cheikh Anta Diop, Angle Canal IV
BP 3304 Dakar, CP 18524, Senegal
Website: www.codesria.org

ISBN: 978-2-86978-506-9

Typesetting: Daouda Thiam
Cover Design: Ibrahima Fofana
Printing: Imprimerie Saint-Paul, Dakar, Senegal

Distributed in Africa by CODESRIA
Distributed elsewhere by African Books Collective, Oxford, UK
Website: www.africanbookscollective.com

The Council for the Development of Social Science Research in Africa (CODESRIA) is an independent organisation whose principal objectives are to facilitate research, promote research-based publishing and create multiple forums geared towards the exchange of views and information among African researchers. All these are aimed at reducing the fragmentation of research in the continent through the creation of thematic research networks that cut across linguistic and regional boundaries.

CODESRIA publishes *Africa Development*, the longest standing Africa based social science journal; *Afrika Zamani*, a journal of history; the *African Sociological Review*; the *African Journal of International Affairs*; *Africa Review of Books* and the *Journal of Higher Education in Africa*. The Council also co-publishes the *Africa Media Review*; *Identity, Culture and Politics: An Afro-Asian Dialogue*; *The African Anthropologist* and the *Afro-Arab Selections for Social Sciences*. The results of its research and other activities are also disseminated through its Working Paper Series, Green Book Series, Monograph Series, Book Series, Policy Briefs and the CODESRIA Bulletin. Select CODESRIA publications are also accessible online at www.codesria.org.

CODESRIA would like to express its gratitude to the Swedish International Development Cooperation Agency (SIDA/SAREC), the International Development Research Centre (IDRC), the Ford Foundation, the MacArthur Foundation, the Carnegie Corporation, the Norwegian Agency for Development Cooperation (NORAD), the Danish Agency for International Development (DANIDA), the French Ministry of Cooperation, the United Nations Development Programme (UNDP), the Netherlands Ministry of Foreign Affairs, the Rockefeller Foundation, FINIDA, the Canadian International Development Agency (CIDA), the Open Society Initiative for West Africa (OSIWA), TrustAfrica, UN/UNICEF, the African Capacity Building Foundation (ACBF) and the Government of Senegal for supporting its research, training and publication programmes.

Contents

Acknowledgements

This book was written as a working paper when I was Senior Research Fellow at the Institute for the Study of Islamic Thought in Africa at Northwestern University. I would like to express my heartfelt thanks to Professor John Hunwick, Director of the Institute, who introduced me to the study of the Arab-Islamic intellectual tradition of sub-Saharan Africa and put his personal library at my disposal during my research work at Northwestern University. This book is dedicated to him. Professor Abdel Wedoud Ould Cheikh, who was at the Institute at the same time as I was, was kind enough to read the first version of this text, making some very useful suggestions, which I so much appreciate. I would also like to thank Achille Mbembe, Mamadou Diouf, Ebrima Sall, Mahmood Mamdani, Habib Kébé, Cheikh Tidiane Fall, Boubacar Diakhaté and Muhamed Sani Umar for their suggestions. Last, but not least, I am grateful to the three anonymous evaluators

Ousmane O. Kane

Note on Transliteration

As this book refers to materials in many languages (Arabic, Hausa, English and French), I have opted for a simplified method of transliteration. The emphatic letters and the lengthy vowels in Arabic words and names are not indicated. When they are proper nouns, I have kept their usual spelling. In general, I have not put Arabic words into the plural. The names of languages or ethnic groups remain invariable (i.e. the Hausa, the Fulani, the *adjami writings*).

1

Introduction

A debate is taking place about post-colonial literature and society in Africa in which writing in English about writing in English or French is pursued without any acknowledgement that a whole world of debate has been going on vigorously and at length in African languages (Graham Furniss, *Poetry, Prose and Popular Culture in Hausa*, p. ix).

For many important cultural purposes, most African intellectuals south of the Sahara are what we can call 'europhone' (Kwame Appiah, *In my Father's House*, p. 4).

In the early 1990s, two books deeply influenced the intellectual debate on the production of knowledge on Africa, on Africanism and Pan-Africanism (Mudimbe 1988 and Appiah 1992), so much so that their authors received, in 1989 and 1993 respectively, the Melville Herskovits Prize from the African Studies Association of North America, which is awarded annually to the best book on Africa written in English. Both authors come from a Christian background, had attended top Western universities (Louvain and Cambridge), teach in two prestigious US universities (Stanford and Princeton) and represented the two dominant intellectual traditions of post-colonial Africa (Anglophone and Francophone). While Appiah's book was based on an in-depth analysis of a limited body of work, mainly Pan-Africanist authors, that of Mudimbe made use of an impressive range of books.

What was more striking as a common denominator between the two authors (which they share with African intellectuals trained in the Western languages) was their very Eurocentric approach to the production of knowledge in Africa and on Africa. Mudimbe argues that the writings that have contributed to the invention and the idea of Africa were, for the most part, produced by Europeans during the colonial period: they formed what he called the colonial library.[1]

As for Appiah, he stated that most of the writings produced in sub-Saharan Africa were in Portuguese, French and English and that consequently most of the intellectuals of sub-Saharan Africa were Europhones (Appiah 1992:4). He added that, historically, the intellectuals of the Third World (including sub-Saharan Africa) were the product of the encounter with the West (Appiah 1992:68).

The 'colonial library' can be traced to the formation of modernity and the Western identity which dates back to the end of the medieval period. In medieval Europe, Latin was the scholarly language par excellence and Christianity the main identity reference. Thanks to the growth of the printing industry and the enormous production of books in vernacular languages (German, English, Polish, Spanish), the European communities gradually acquired a national identity that supplanted the religious one (Anderson, *passim*). As they acquired these new identities, which were an important dimension of Western modernity, they also constructed the identity of 'savages': people who were not Western (Hall 1996). The accounts of travellers and the testimonies of explorers and missionaries, as well as writings by the thinkers of the Enlightenment, contributed to the idea that there was a relationship of radical otherness between the West and the Rest.

In the case of Africa, Mudimbe (1994, *passim)* tried to question the very idea of the continent that the social sciences[2] had developed. To illustrate the controversial nature of the term 'Africa' which originally designated a Roman province of Northern Africa, Mudimbe analyzed works of art and Greek texts about the black people, as well as accounts by European travellers, missionaries and explorers. He stated that the writings constituted the nucleus of a 'library' that has created extremely simplistic, if not racist, representations of a mosaic of peoples and places in Africa, whose culture, ecology, modes of social organization and political economy differ so greatly that one wonders whether, apart from its geographical location, the term Africa makes any sense at all.[3]

During the colonial period, this embryo of a library was reinforced by anthropologists and other colonial writers whose aim was to help create governable subjects (Mudimbe 1994:xii). Later, the library was enriched by the writings of Africanists (non-African researchers working on Africa). This expanded library shaped, according to Mudimbe, an epistemological territory inhabited by concepts and worldviews inherited from the West. Even during the post-colonial period, neither the Africanists nor the Africans who were preaching the authenticity of Africa, and still less the Afrocentrists, were able to break out of the extremely schematic and simplistic representation of Africa that the Western epistemological order had invented (Mudimbe 1988:x; 1994:xv). According to Mudimbe, 'the European interpreters, like the African analysts, used categories and conceptual systems that stemmed from the Western epistemological order' (1988:x).

This is very much the case for Appiah who makes a powerful critique of Pan-Africanist thinking by deconstructing the myth that was at its heart: the illusion that the Africans constituted a race, the black race, whose members had common biological and cultural characteristics that distinguished them from members of other races. This illusion, and here we come to the Western epistemological order proposed by Mudimbe, is the effect of racist ideologies that were deeply rooted in the nineteenth century West, during which most of the Pan-African thinkers were born. And Appiah added that Africans who were to become future leaders like Senghor, Kenyatta and Nkrumah, although born in a context of less conflictual race relations, embraced the notion that race was a reality and must consequently be 'an organizing principle of political solidarity'. Numerous intellectuals among the most erudite have not been able to question this idea of a monolithic, homogenous Africa created by the colonial library. The categorization of Africa into ethnic and racial identities is another legacy of the colonial library that the anthropologists have taken some time to overcome and its absurdity is evident in recent works on the ethnogenesis of African populations.

It is time to rethink the quasi-monopoly claimed by Western languages and epistemological order in the process of making African reality intelligible (Copans 1993). This is not only because of the numerous recent works that shed light on the vigorous written and oral debates in non-Western languages, but also because there is a common post-colonial space of meaning shared by Europhone intellectuals and non-Europhone intellectuals, as well as intellectuals who result from a mixture of the two.

Moreover, apart from the colonial library, there are other libraries, including the Islamic one, to which numerous intellectuals have contributed, who cannot be described as Europhones. There is not only one epistemological order, but several 'spaces of meaning' in Africa, as Zaki Laidi (1998) would say. The Islamic space of meaning (Kepel 2000:74) is structured by Islamic beliefs and practices (esoteric and exoteric Islamic knowledge and religious practices such as praying, fasting, proselytizing, pilgrimages to the tombs of saints). This space of meaning has had considerable influence on populations, especially those in African areas that have been strongly Islamized. The formation of this space of meaning took place over a thousand years of slow Islamization, during which Arabic language and culture acquired currency in numerous parts of sub-Saharan Africa.

The aim of this book is to provide a framework for the creation of a CODESRIA Pan-African research group on intellectuals whom I label 'non-Europhone'. It addresses the intellectual contribution of scholars whom I consider as intellectuals because they come from a scholarly tradition and formulate claims couched in Islamic political terms. These are the two major themes of this book.

First, I shall consider the research that has been carried out on the Islamic library to show that a substantial number of intellectuals in sub-Saharan Africa have written in Arabic or in *d'jami* (African languages written with the Arabic script). This sub-Saharan African Islamic library is made up of personal accounts about Africa by Arab authors that go back to the medieval period, classical works on Islamic knowledge written by Arab authors but which have circulated in sub-Saharan Africa, and texts produced by African scholars. A large proportion consists of manuscripts to whose collection I devote an important part of this paper. I also deal with the networks for training intellectuals in the Arab-Islamic tradition, as well as the language used by these intellectuals to criticize the African pre-colonial political and social order and successfully to mobilize support in the larger society in order to transform that order.

I also consider the 'mixing process' which created intellectuals drawing on different traditions, while maintaining their allegiance to Islam. To conclude, I identify certain fields of research on non-Europhone intellectuals and knowledge outside the Islamic tradition, as well as the phenomenon of intellectual cross-fertilization.

2

The Islamic Library in Sub-Saharan Africa

Spoken only in the Arabian peninsula, Arabic was, in the pre-Islamic period, the language of the tribe of the Prophet Muhammad. With the expansion of Islam, it became in 2009 the language of 300 million Arabs, from Arabia to North Africa, and the liturgical language of a billion and a half Muslims from Indonesia to Senegal. In North Africa, which had been thoroughly Christianized[4] before the advent of Islam, the local population adopted not only the Islamic religion but also the Arabic language and culture. So they are called Arabized Arabs (*mustá riba*), as opposed to Arabizing Arabs (*ariba*), who are the Arabophone populations of the Arabian peninsula.

Judging by the number of colleges and other celebrated centres of learning established in Northern Africa (Qarawiyyin in Morocco, Zeytuna in Tunisia, Al-Azhar in Egypt), as well as their lively intellectual tradition during the medieval period, it has to be recognized that the Arabs and Muslims made a remarkable contribution to Islamic civilization and to medieval civilization in general. There was no field of knowledge that Muslim scholars had not investigated between the eighth and the fifteenth centuries. They contributed to philosophy, astronomy, mathematics, geography, medicine, pharmacy and chemistry (Kader 1996; Djebbar 2001). In 815, the library of Baghdad, capital of the Muslim eastern empire, contained about a million works. That of Cordoba in Spain comprised 400,000 manuscripts (Kader 1996:148) — more than all the works of the other Western European libraries combined. Saharan and sub-Saharan Africans participated in this Islamic civilization, not only as consumers but also as contributors. This African contribution to civilization and, above all, to the intellectual history of Islam was neglected for a long time. It was only in the post-colonial period, and particularly in the two decades from 1990 to 2010, that considerable efforts have been made to reconstitute the African Islamic library and to make it accessible to a Europhone public.

In contrast with North Africa, where Islamization and Arabization were rapid and almost total, sub-Saharan Africa was not entirely Islamized, nor even really Arabized. Africa was not wholly Islamized because the Islamic expansion in sub-Sahara stopped at the equator. Even if Muslim communities are to be found on the eastern coast of Africa, they remain minorities in their respective countries. Sub-Saharan Africa was not really Arabized either (except for Sudan), because most Muslims, even if they used Arabic as a liturgical language, expressed themselves in African languages in everyday life.

The writings of Arab intellectuals are relatively well-known in the Arab world as well as in the West because numerous reference works exist in Arabic and in Western languages. In the European languages, there are two outstanding reference works: *The Encyclopaedia of Islam* and the *Geschichte Der Arabishen Litteratur*. The former, of which there are two editions, and which exists in both French and English versions, covers essential aspects of the history, geography, philosophy, theology and culture of a large part of the Islamic world. The first edition was completed in 1938 and the second edition in 2005, and have greatly contributed to improving our knowledge of Arabic, Turkish and Persian intellectual history.

The compiler of the second important reference work, which is in German (there is now an Arabic translation) was Carl Brockelman. It was comprised of three volumes published in the 1940s (Brockelman 1937-1942). They were then followed by two supplementary volumes, published under the title *Geschichte der Arabishen Litteratur Supplementhanden* (Brockelman 1943-1949).

As for the reference works in Arabic, there are of course a large number of them. Two examples of major biographical dictionaries are the *Al-A ʿlam* of Khayr al-Din Al-Zirikli (1979) and the *Mu ʿjam al-mu'allifin* of ʿUmar R. Kahhala (1957).

Entitled the *Biographical Dictionary of Arab authors, Arabists, and Orientalists*, Al-Zirikli's work, which was first published in 1927, has since come out in three updated editions, in 1957, 1969 and 1979. It comprises eight volumes and contains biographical information on many Arab and Orientialist authors and on their works.

The Mu*ʿjam al-mu'allifin'* of ʿUmar R. Kahhala (1957) is another encyclopaedic reference work on Arabic writings. In 14 volumes, the *Mʿjam*, as its title indicates, aims at giving maximum information about works written in Arabic, their authors, the genealogy of these authors and their fields of specialization.

However, consultation of these four major reference works gives the impression that sub-Saharan Africa has not contributed to the intellectual history of the Muslim world. The *Encyclopaedia of Islam* focuses on the so-called central Muslim world. The *Geschichte* devotes only five pages to sub-Saharan Africa. Al-Zirikli and Kahhala barely cite authors from sub-Saharan Africa. This means that most of sub-Saharan African Arabists are not only unknown to the Europhones, but also to a good number of Arab and orientalist compilers. And yet the external and internal Arabic and *djami* sources are very useful for studying the history, philosophy and sociology of the Islamized part of Africa during the second millennium. These external Arab sources consist of testimonies from medieval Arab authors and have been put at the disposal of the Europhone public through the works of Prince Yusuf Kamal, Father J. Cuoq, John Hopkins and Nehemia Levtzion.

Compiled by a team of researchers from different nationalities, the *Monumenta Carthographica Africae and Aegypti* of Yusuf Kamal constitutes the greatest cartographical work ever undertaken, in terms of its broad range. It reproduces all the maps that concern Africa, however remotely (Sizgin in *Introduction to Kamal* 1987). Furthermore, the *Monumenta* includes an exhaustive inventory of written texts in Greek, Latin, Arabic and other medieval European languages that concern Africa, from Pharaonic Egypt to the arrival of the Portuguese in 1434. But up until recently, it was very little cited, for two main reasons. First, because only 100 copies of the first edition were produced by Brill between 1926 and 1951, of which 75 were offered to libraries. Second, the 16 volumes were large and weighty: they measured 75 x 60 centimetres and weighed between 15 and 20 kilograms each (Sizgin in *Introduction to Kamal* 1987). Only in 1987 was a second, relatively accessible edition of *Monumenta* edited by Fuat Sizgin (Kamal 1987). So, for a long time, the *Monumenta* was very seldom cited in African historiography (Mauny, in Cuoq 1975:xi-xii).

The second, more accessible work was entitled *Recueil des sources arabes concernant l'Afrique occidentale du VIIe siècle au XVe siècle.* This book was the result of the labours of Father Joseph Cuoq who lived for many years in West Africa. It was published in 1975 and covered all sources concerning West Africa, that is, the area to the west of the Nile and south of the Sahara. The book, which listed 25 writers not mentioned in the *Monumenta,* only dealt with Arabic sources. It provided crucially important testimonies on the medieval states of Ghana, Mali, Songhai, Kanem, Borno, etc.

As for the third work, it has a rather more complex history. It was the University of Ghana that took the initiative, in 1956, during the national effervescence on the eve of independence of this former British colony, to collect the material. John Fage established a provisional list of materials based mainly on the *Monumenta* (Hopkins and Levtzion, ix). Witold Rajkowski of London University translated a third of this material but died before he could complete it. This was then carried on by John Hopkins who, with Nehemia Levtzion, edited the translation and published it in 1981 under the title *Corpus of Early Arabic Sources of West African History.* The Corpus listed 66 Arab authors writing between the ninth and seventeenth centuries, including Ibn Batuta. They supplied both first-hand and second-hand information on important periods of West Africa history. Apart from these older external sources, on which we have a certain amount of information, there are other internal sources in Arabic or in *djami*, upon which some researchers have been working for some time.

The Muslims of sub-Saharan Africa began producing texts in Arabic in the medieval era. (The earliest known black African scholar who wrote in Arabic is Abu Ishaq Ibrahim al-Kanemi, who flourished around 1200 (Hunwick 1995:1). However, for a long time the work of these writers was not seriously studied. Several kinds of prejudice are responsible for this. First, the European Orientalists, as well as the Arab authors, who possessed the necessary linguistic abilities to study these texts, found the erudition of these writers of little interest and decided – with a few exceptions – that there was no point in pursuing them.

Second, the African researchers and Africanists specializing in the social sciences, either because they considered the Islamization of sub-Saharan Africa to be superficial or because they were mostly ignorant of the existence of a literature in the Arabic language or in *djami*, did not integrate these works into their studies. One consequence for the historiography of Africa, is that there are few historians interested in sources in the Arabic language or in the *djami* because they assume that most of the sources on Africa's history are either written sources in Western languages, or oral ones.

However, over the last few decades many commendable initiatives have been taken to reconstitute the Islamic library. They have taken the form of cataloguing and publishing collections of manuscripts in Arabic or *djami* and, to a certain extent, the translation of some of them into Western languages.

As far as the collection and cataloguing of the manuscripts is concerned, the work carried out has varied from country to country. In Chad, Cameroon and Niger, there has been no rigorous work done in listing the manuscripts in Arabic or in *djami* (Hunwick 1995:XII), whereas in Mauritania, Senegal, Nigeria and Mali, considerable progress has been made in listing these texts.

The situation of Mauritania differs from the rest of West Africa in that it is located in Western Sahara (between the Arab world and the Maghreb) and its population is largely Arabophone. The Arabic Islamic intellectual history of Mauritania, one of the richest of West Africa, was very little known for a long time, even in the Arab world (Stewart, et al. 1990:79). Now there are three reference works which have helped to make this history known: that of Al-Burtuli (1727/28-1805), called *Fath al-Shakur* (Al-Burtuli 1981), which was translated into French by Chouki al-Hamel (1992); the *Wasit* of Muhammad al-Amin Al-Shinguiti, written at the beginning of the twentieth century; and the more recent *Bilad al-Shinqit* of Al-Khalil al-Nahwi (1987).

In addition to biographical dictionaries, several inventories have been made in Mauritania, of which three deserve mention. The first is the provisional catalogue drawn up by Adam Heymouski, former curator of the Royal Swedish Library and Moukhar Ould Hamidoun, doyen of the contemporary Mauritanian historians (Heymouski and Ould Hamidoun 1965-1966). Only a few examples of this catalogue were printed in Arabic. It included a phonetic transcription, and, in alphabetical order, a list of 425 authors among the best known in Mauritania, as well as some 2,000 works by these authors, with a brief description of the theme of their manuscripts.

Twenty years later, Ulrich Von Rebstock published the *Rohkatalog der Arabischen Handschriften in Mauretanien,* the result of the work of a team at the University of Tübingen, together with the Mauritanian Institute for Scientific Research. This catalogue, which was written entirely in Latin characters, made a remarkable contribution to the list of Mauritanian Arab manuscripts. There are 2,239 listed manuscripts (Stewart 1990:180) of which the oldest is by an eleventh century author (Ould Cheikh 1987:111). They come from some hundred libraries and manuscript collections and cover the main regions of Mauritania, as well as a wide range of subjects. Sixty percent of the texts are about the following: *ad'iyya* (invocations), *adhkar* (litanies), *fatawi* (legal opinions), *fiqh* (jurisprudence), *hadith* (science of traditions), *mawa'iz* (exhortations), *nawazil* (juridical affairs), *Qur'an* (the Koran), *sira* (biography of the Prophet), tasawwuf (Sufism), *tawhid* (theology), *usul* (sources of law). Then there are linguistic and literary studies: *adab* (literature), *'arud* (metrics), *bayan* (rhetoric), *lugha* (language), *mantiq* (logic), *nahw* (grammar), *shi'r* (poetry). Finally, there are texts listed under the following themes: political ethics, astronomy-astrology, geography, mathematics, magic, medicine, and agriculture (Ould Cheikh 1987:111). This work is more detailed than the *Catalogue provisoire,* featuring as it does the name of the author, the title of the manuscript, the place where it has been filmed, the theme, the date of completion, as well as the library where it is located (Ould Cheikh 1987:110).

The third important work in this listing of Mauritanian manuscripts is the *Catalogue de manuscripts arabes* of the Mauritanian Institute for Scientific Research which, according to its chief compiler, Stewart (1990), constitutes the most complete study of Arabic literature and Islamic studies in Mauritania. Between 1975 and 1990, this Institute collected and bought 3,100 manuscripts in order to establish a national manuscript collection.

In 1988-89, these manuscripts were catalogued on the basis of bilingual data (Arabic/English). The compilers adopted a system of transliteration taking into account the specificity of Hasaniyya, the Arabic dialect spoken in Mauritania. The total volume of the catalogued manuscripts (some 1,546 pages of entries, plus 200 pages of index) is available for consultation at the Mauritanian Institute for Scientific Research and at the University of Illinois at Urbana Champaign (Stewart 1990:180). The themes covered generally reflect those of the Arabic literature of West Africa: a large number of works on jurisprudence, Sufism, the Arabic language, Koranic studies, literature, science of traditions and theology. To a lesser extent, they include texts on invocation, history, logic, ethics, mathematics, astronomy/astrology, medicine, esoterism, encyclopaedias, pedagogy, geography (Stewart 1990:183). According to Abdel Weddoud Ould Cheikh, it is in the towns of Shinqit, Tishit and Boutlimit that the most important collections of manuscripts were found. However, because of the rural exodus, the greater parts of the libraries that had been based in these towns are now in Nouakchott (personal communication 2001).

There has also been much recording and cataloguing of manuscripts in Mali. First, there was the work undertaken on the Umarian library of Ségou, known as the Archinard Collection (Fonds Archinard in French). The collection was seized by the French commander Achinard during the French conquest of the empire of El-Hadji Omar Tall and is now located in the National Library at Paris. An inventory of its contents was carried out by Ghali, Mahibou and Brenner (1985).

It is above all, thanks to the sponsorship of the Al-Furqan Foundation, based in London, that the recording of the manuscript heritage has created renewed interest in Mali and elsewhere in West Africa. Established at the beginning of the 1990s by Sheikh Ahmad Zaki Yamani, the former Saudi Oil Minister, the *Al-Furqan li-Ihya al-Turath al-Islami* Foundation, as its name indicates, aims at rekindling the Islamic cultural heritage. It sponsored the publication of an encyclopaedia in four volumes covering the collections of manuscripts in most of the Muslim countries (Roper 1994). Entitled *The World Survey of Islamic Manuscripts,* the encyclopaedia identified the public and private collections of 'Islamic manuscripts' in the languages of Muslim peoples: Arabic, Persian, Turkish, Asian and African languages. The World Survey provides the locations, conditions of access as well as an overview of the number and themes of the manuscripts preserved in those collections. *The World Survey* includes many entries on sub-Saharan African countries.

Over the last decade and following the publication of *The World Survey,* the Al-Furqan Foundation has produced some 30 detailed catalogues in Arabic, with special emphasis on non-catalogued collections. These catalogues, of which almost half concern certain African countries, including Senegal (Kane 1997) and Nigeria (Muhammad Hunwick 1995, 1997, 2001), drew the attention of researchers to a large body of unpublished material, of which Mali takes the lion's share. Collaboration between the Al-Furqan Foundation and the Ahmad Baba Centre for Research and Historical Documentation at Timbuktu (CEDRAB) has made it possible to publish five volumes in Arabic between 1995 and 1998 that list the

9,000 manuscripts that constitute part of CEDRAB's collection. The first volume of 1,500 manuscripts was compiled by Sidi Amar Ould Eli and edited by Julian Johansen (1995). The second, third and fourth volumes, each listing 1,500 manuscripts and published in 1996, 1997 and 1998 respectively were compiled by a team of librarians of CEDRAB and edited by Abd Al-Muhsin Al-Abbas of the Al-Furqan Foundation (CEDRAB librarians, Al-Abbas 1996, 1997, 1998). The fifth volume, which is larger than the others, was compiled and edited by a team of CEDRAB librarians, and features 3,000 manuscripts (CEDRAB librarians 1998). Each of these documents was published with several indexes: of titles of manuscripts, names of authors, themes and names of transcribers, so that the contents of the work can be rapidly consulted.

The collaboration between Al-Furqan and the Mamma Haidara Commemorative Library of Timbuktu has also enabled the publication, in three volumes, of a catalogue of the manuscripts contained in this library, which was established more than five hundred years ago and is currently based at Timbuktu. Compiled by Abdelkadir Mamma Haidara and edited by Ayman Fuad Sayyid, the catalogue of this library's bequests lists 3,000 manuscripts (Haidara and Ayman 2000).

The Malian manuscripts can be divided into two categories: The first category includes texts in various fields of Islamic knowledge. The second category is made up of historical documents. In the first category are found texts on (*adab*), jurisprudence (*fiqh*), Sufism (*tasawwuf*) and the Koranic sciences ('*ulum al-qur'an*) predominate, but there are also texts on the *ijaza* (diplomas or authorizations to transmit exoteric or initiation knowledge), ethics (*akhlaq*), invocations (*ad'iyya*), sources of religion (*usul al-din*), theory of law (*usul al-fiqh*), genealogies (*ansab*), history (*ta'rikh*), Koranic exegesis (*tafsir*), theology (*tawhid* and '*aqa'id*), science of traditions (*hadith*), mathematics (*hisab*), politics (*siyasa*), biographies (*tarajim*), the biography of the Prophet (*sira nabawiyya*), morphology and syntax (*nahw, sarf*), medicine (*tibb*), metrics ('arud), astronomy (*falak*), chemistry (*kimiya*), logic (*mantiq*), exhortations (*wa'dh wa irshad*). Their authors are Arabs and Africans.

Historical documents form a substantial part of these libraries (one out of three manuscripts in the Mamma Haidara Commemorative Library). They are the work of African writers and give information about social life and the customs of the peoples of the region, legal opinions (*fatwa*), financial transactions of all kinds, relationships between the *ulemas* and the merchants in different periods of history, as well as the relationships between the peoples of the region and those of other Muslim countries, like Morocco, Tunisia and Libya.

The many manuscripts found in Mali are mostly the heritage of great intellectual centres like Djenné, Timbuktu, Gao, etc. Gao (or Kawkaw) was, according to the Arab author Muhallabi, who died in 990 (Cuoq 1975:77), the capital of a small Islamic principality of the Niger Bend during the tenth century. It became a flourishing commercial, political and intellectual centre during the medieval period and attained its apogee as the capital of the Songhai empire under the reign of the Askia dynasty (sixteenth century). Its most famous ruler, Askia Muhammad Touré, went on pilgrimage to Mecca in 1496 and visited Egypt. He was named Caliph (Muslim sovereign) of the Sudan (country of the black people) by the Abassid Caliph al-Mutawakkil and by the Sharifian Ruler of Mecca (Hiskett 1985:35). As proved in many texts by Muslim scholars of the period which have come down to us, Askia Muhammad greatly contributed to spreading the culture and the teaching of Islam. He consulted two renowned Arab scholars on how to govern his country in conformity with Islamic precepts. One of them was Abd al-Karim al-Maghili (who died in 1504), who replied to Askia Muhammad's questions in the form of *fatwa*. The questions and responses have been translated into English (Hunwick 1985).

Among the contributions of Al-Maghili to sub-Saharan Islam was the fundamental idea that in each century a Muslim reformer, versed in the religious sciences, would appear and lay down what was allowed, forbid what was illicit, preside over peoples' destinies and settle their quarrels (Hiskett 1985:36). This idea influenced many political movements led by Muslim scholars in the seventeenth, eighteenth and nineteenth centuries, some of which led to the creation of Islamic theocracies.[5]

The other scholar consulted by Askia Muhammad Touré was Jalal al-Din Suyuti (who died in 1505). One of the greatest scholars of the Arab-Muslim world of his time, Al-Suyuti is reported to have written several hundred treatises. There is no evidence that he visited sub-Saharan Africa, but we know that he met Askia Muhammad in Cairo during the latter's pilgrimage to Mecca and that he subsequently exchanged correspondence with him, providing him with advice on the administration of Islamic law (Hiskett 1985:37).

Djenné is another great Islamic centre in the Mali of today. Although there is not full agreement about when it was founded, we know that it was one of the major centres of Arabo-Islamic culture before Timbuktu. According to al-Saʿdi, when the twenty-sixth sovereign of Djenné converted to Islam during the thirteenth century, the town already had 4,200 Muslim *ulemas* (Hunwick 1999b:19, Touré 1999:1).

As for the town of Timbuktu, which was originally a Tuareg encampment (at the end of the eleventh century), in the fifteenth century it became an important hub in trans-Saharan trade and a great Islamic centre. It had flourishing colleges – in the medieval meaning of the term, in other words, communities of teachers and students living together with the objective of transmitting or acquiring religious knowledge (Hiskett 1985:40-41) and enjoying royal privileges (Touré 1999:3). The best known of these colleges (Djingerey-ber, Sankoré and the Oratory of

Sidi-Yahya) were already operating at the beginning of the fourteenth century. The Djingerey-ber College was founded between 1325 and 1330 by the Emperor of Mali on his return from a pilgrimage to Mecca (Touré 1999:3). Under the leadership of the Sanhaja Berbers, Sankoré was built between 1325 and 1433 (Touré 1999:3). Finally, the Oratory of Sidi Yahya or the mosque of Mohamed Naddah was built right at the beginning of the fifteenth century (Touré 1999:3). These colleges maintained relationships with other universities in North Africa and Egypt which recognized their curriculum and their authorization to transmit knowledge (Touré 1999:1). They were to a large extent designed on the model of Al-Azhar (Hiskett 1985:41).

The two richest chronicles on the history of the region, *Tarikh al-Sudan* and *Tarikh al-Fattash*, were written by scholars of Timbuktu. Translated in 1913 by Octave Houdas and Maurice Delafosse, Mahmud Ka'ti's *Tarikh al-Fattash fi akhbar al-buldan wa al-juyush wa akabir al-nas* (The researcher's chronicle, serving the history of the towns, the armies and the principal personalities) is a basic source for the history of the great empires of the Western Sudan (Ly 1972:471).

The other work, which is by Abdarrahman al-Sa'di, is entitled *Tarikh al-Sudan*, Sudan being the name given by Arab authors to the regions south of the Sahara. When Al-Sa'di used the term Al-Sudan he referred to sub-Saharan Africa and more particularly to the region of the Middle Niger. The book is a monumental account of the history of Timbuktu and Djenné, describing in detail the origin of the Sonni dynasty, as well as that of the Askia, who succeeded it. The *Tarikh al-Sudan* also contains a fascinating analysis of the decline of the Songhai empire in the aftermath of the Moroccan Invasion. It was translated into two Western languages: into French by Octave Houdas and Maurice Delafosse at the beginning of the twentieth century (Al-Sa'di 1964), and into English by Hunwick (1999b) who has translated the essential part of the text. Hunwick's translation is accompanied by notes that include the latest findings of African historiography and it concludes with the collapse of the Songhai empire in 1613, that is, two decades after the Moroccan invasion. In an annex to Hunwick's work there are some important documents that have also been translated, including the description of West Africa by Hasan b. Muhammad al-Wazzan al-Zayyati, more often known as Leo Africanus, correspondence between the Moroccan sovereign Al-Mansur and the Songhai sovereigns, and personal accounts of the Moroccan invasion of the Songhai empire.

Senegal is another country that has a rich Arab-Islamic intellectual tradition, with numerous colleges in the pre-colonial period. During the 1930s, the French colonial administration supported the idea of collecting and interpreting historical knowledge about the regions that it controlled. Thus, numerous colonial administrators took to compiling and translating sources of information in Arabic and *djami*. In some cases, historical sources were compiled at the request of colonial administrators, for example the two manuscripts edited by Siré Abbas Soh at the request of Maurice Delafosse (1870-1926) and translated with the help of Henry Gaden (1867-1939) (Pondopoulo 1993:96).

The creation of an Islamic studies department at the French Institute for Black Africa (IFAN) also contributed to the effort to collect Arabic sources. One of its directors, Vincent Monteil, drew up a provisional list of Arab-African manuscripts which was published in 1965, part of which is dedicated to Senegalese manuscripts (Monteil 1965:539-541 and 1966:671-673). After independence, IFAN was renamed the Fundamental Institute for Black Africa and is now affiliated to the University of Dakar. A great effort to collect and catalogue Arabic and *djami* manuscripts has been made by the IFAN researchers who published, in 1966, a *Catalogue des manuscrits de l'IFAN*, listing the Vieillard Gaden, Brévié, Figaret, Shaykh Musa Kamara and Cremer collections. These collections contain manuscripts in Arabic, Fula and Voltaic languages (Diallo et al. 1966).

Amar Samb was among these researchers – as well as being the director of IFAN – and he was the author of a work devoted essentially to the contribution of Senegal to Arabic literature. He reviewed a good dozen of what he called literary schools established by Senegalese scholars who had taught the Arabic language to thousands of disciples and made a significant contribution to Arabic literature. He cited the schools of Dakar, Thiès, Kaolack, Saint Louis, Touba, Louga, Ziguinchor and others (Samb 1972). His work was completed by Ousmane Kane and John Hunwick who listed, in Senegambia alone, more than a hundred authors and their works, which were mostly in Arabic (Kane and Hunwick 2002 a,b,c,d).

Another IFAN researcher was El-hadji Rawane Mbaye, formerly director of the Islamic Institute of Dakar and coordinator of the pilgrimage to Mecca up until 2001. He spent most of his professional life studying the Arabic literature of Senegal and was the co-author, with Babacar Mbaye, of a supplement to the catalogue of IFAN manuscripts (Mbaye and Mbaye 1975), as well as of two doctoral theses, one a round-up of Islamic teaching in Senegal (Mbaye 1975) and the other a biography of the Senegalese scholar Al-Hadji Malick Sy (who died in 1922) as well as a translation of two of his writings (Mbaye 1993).

More recently, Thierno Kâ and Khadim Mbacké (1994) produced a new catalogue of IFAN manuscripts that listed recently collected materials and was mainly concerned with Senegambian authors. Khadim Mbacké (1996) has translated into French a hagiography of Ahmadou Bamba entitled *Minan al-baqi al-qadim fi sirat Shaykh al-khadim*, written by his son, Bachirou Mbacké.

However, it has to be said that there is little interest on the part of social science researchers in this poorly understood part of African history. The valuable work of translating and editing carried out by a group of researchers from the Centre National de la Recherche Scientifique (CNRS), IFAN and the Cheikh Anta Diop University is an important exception. It features the masterpiece of the Senegalese scholar Sheikh Muusa Kamara entitled *Zuhur al-basatin fi tarikh al-sawadin* (Flowers from the gardens in the history of the black people), an alternative title of which is *intisar al-mawtur fi tarikh bilad Futa Tur* (Triumph of the oppressed through the study of the history of Futa Tur). The first volume of this work (out of the four yet to appear) was coordinated by J. Schmitz and published in 1999.

Like the great historical works such as *Tarikh al-Sudan* and *Tarikh al-Fattash*, the *Zuhur al-basatin* is very long (1,700 pages), written partly in Arabic and partly in *djami*. It constitutes a major source of information on economic and social life in the valley of the Senegal river, giving first-hand accounts of political organization and land tenure in the Middle Valley of the Senegalese River, particularly in the nineteenth and twentieth centuries. When it appeared, researchers once again realized the utility of Arabic and *djami* sources in reconstituting the history of West Africa. Important as it is, however, the *Zuhur al-basatin* is not the only work of Sheikh Muusa Kamara. He is also the author of various texts in Arabic and Pulaar on such different fields as history, geography, the hydrology of the Senegal river from Guinea to Saint Louis, literature, sociology, anthropology, jurisprudence, traditional medicine, Sufism, etc. (interview with Abdou Malal Diop 1999).

As in Senegal, the colonial administrators of Nigeria were also interested in historical sources and made a considerable attempt to collect and translate them. However, it was in the post-colonial period that really serious efforts were made to reconstitute the sources in non-Western languages. Among the many bodies that were involved were the Jamaʿat Nasr al-Islam (JNI), the Northern History Research Scheme, the Centre for Islamic Studies of Uthman Dan Fodio University and Arewa House of Kaduna.

The Jamaʿat Nasr al-Islam was founded by Ahmadu Bello, Prime Minister of Northern Nigeria between 1960 and 1966, with the idea of federating all Muslims who were mostly members of Sufi brotherhoods and antagonistic to each other. Striving to unify them on the basis of their common heritage of the jihad of the nineteenth century led by his great grandfather Uthman Dan Fodio, Bello encouraged the translation and publication of writings by the intellectuals who had led the jihad (Paden 1986:550-551).

Moreover, on the initiative of Abdullahi Smith, professor of history at the University of Ibadan, then at the Ahmadu Bello University, a new generation of historians, mainly Nigerians, tried to break with colonial historiography, starting with re-readings of the jihad of Uthman Dan Fodio. This generation of students of Abdullahi Smith, among whom were Yusufu Bala Usman, Abdullahi Mahadi, Murray Last and Mahmud Tukur, exploited a substantial amount of Arab sources. The historical research laboratory, called the Northern History Research Scheme of the Ahmadu Bello University in Zaria, participated in this effort to promote the sources in non-Western languages in the history of Nigeria.

Along the same lines, the Centre for Islamic Studies of the Usmane Dan Fodiyo University of Sokoto listed some 300 dissertations and theses on Islam in Nigeria that have been presented in Nigerian and other universities (Sifawa 1988). They are mainly written in English but some are in Hausa and Arabic. They cover various fields, including general works on Islam, its expansion in the different regions of Nigeria, the biographies of some Islamic personalities, in particular the Fodiawa (disciples and descendants of Uthman Dan Fodio). There are some fifty translations from Arabic into English, and rather fewer into Hausa, of commentaries and critical analyses of the thoughts of certain authors. The whole is dominated by the three leading Fodiawa, Uthman Dan Fodio, Abdullahi Dan Fodio and Muhammad Bello. Finally, to conclude the contributions on Nigeria, the work of two authors, Ali Abu Bakr and Kabiru Galadanci, should be noted. They have created syntheses, analyzing works in Arabic and listing their authors (Abu Bakr 1972; Galadanci 1982).

At the same time, the Arabic Literature of Africa Project, directed by Sean O'Fahey and John Hunwick should be mentioned. Noting that the Arabic literature of Africa is very little known, these two authors, with the help of collaborators in Africa and elsewhere, undertook the ambitious project of listing all the authors who contributed to the Islamic scholarly tradition of sub-Saharan Africa, as well as their works (in Arabic, Pulaar, Swahili, Hausa, etc). This work has resulted in the production of two volumes dedicated respectively to the Nilotic Sudan up until 1900 (O'Fahey 1994) and central Sudan (Hunwick 1995). A third publication in two volumes, covering Swahili literature and East Africa, and a fourth one on West Sudan have been completed and are in the press. Two more volumes should terminate the series and these will be dedicated to Nilotic Sudan and Western Sahara respectively. The volumes on the Arabic literature of Africa are mainly concerned with texts in Arabic and, to a lesser degree, in *a'jami*. As a didactic tool, modelled on the *Geschichte* of Carl Brockelman, *Arabic Literature of Africa* features the authors, their writings and the scholarly tradition to which they belong. In the same spirit, J. Hunwick and S. O'Fahey created in 1999 the Institute for the Study of Islamic Thought in Africa (ISITA), based at Northwestern University, Evanston, USA, which strives to mobilise a community of researchers around programmes for pre- and post-doctoral fellowships, conferences and publications. This institute constitutes the beginning of an effort to study systematically the Islamic thought of sub-Saharan Africa.

Two journals have made a decisive contribution to reconstituting the Islamic library. One is *Islam et Sociétés au Sud du Sahara* which, published by the Maison des Sciences de l'Homme in Paris, is bilingual (English/French) and the product of the tropical Islamic laboratory of that institution. Founded and directed by Jean-Louis Triaud, this journal was started following an international conference on 'Religious Agents South of the Sahara', organized by the laboratory. Over the years, *Islam et Sociétés* has produced 20 issues and created a space for exchanges between African, American, European and Asian researchers on sub-Saharan Islam and become a valuable tool for sub-Saharan researchers and scholars of comparative religion. Each issue contains, in an annex, a bibliography of recent books and articles on Muslim African societies. *Islam et Sociétés* also publishes many reviews accounts of unpublished texts (B.A. and Ph.D. theses presented in various universities and difficult of access). It features many critical studies of Arabic sources and Arabized intellectuals of sub-Saharan Africa.

The second journal is *Sudanic Africa: A Journal of Historical Sources,* of which there are both printed and electronic versions (http://www.hf-fak-uib.no/smi/sa).[6] It was created in 1990 by John Hunwick and Sean O'Fahey. Its main function is to publish original documents in Arabic or African languages on the history and culture of Saharan and sub-Saharan Africa. Like *Islam et Sociétés, Sudanic Africa* has also published numerous biographies of Arabized intellectuals of sub-Saharan Africa in the eleven issues that have appeared so far.

After this review of the state of research on these Arabists in Africa, let us now look at the historical origins of this intellectual tradition.

3

Origins of the Islamic Scholarly Tradition in Sub-Saharan Africa

The growth of literacy in Arabic and *ajami* in sub-Saharan Africa is closely linked to the expansion of Islam and the trans-Saharan trade, which was the main vector of Islamic expansion. Islam began to penetrate West Africa in the ninth century. But it was around the eleventh century that the elites of many urban chiefdoms and empires in West African Sahel became Islamized through contact with North African and Saharan traders (Hunwick 1997:5; Triaud 1998:10 and 6, Hiskett 1985:19-42).

The growth of the trans-Saharan trade and the expansion of Islam brought about a transformation of the West African societies that were subjected to their influence. The process was reinforced by a new form of state that developed in West Africa from the eighth to the sixteenth centuries. It was described by Bathily (1994:44-51) as the military-merchant state. In contrast to stateless societies (Horton 1985:911 et seq., 113 et seq.) which were based on agriculture and, to a lesser extent, on livestock, and the traditional African state based on agricultural, pastoral and agro-pastoral activities, the political economy of the military-merchant state was based mainly on the tertiary sector (Bathily 1994:44) and its expansion was a critical period in the growth of literacy in Arabic. The military-merchant state was dominated by three types of elite: military, commercial and religious, each of which carried out a vital function for its development. The military aristocracy, often originating from the political elite of the old traditional states, specialized in weaponry and was responsible for security. The commercial elite, which operated along the trans-Saharan trade routes and kept constant contact with the great commercial and cultural centres of North Africa – in Qayrawan, Gadames, Tripoli – produced the wealth necessary for the development of the state. The religious elite ensured its legitimization, while taking over the production, reproduction and distribution of spiritual goods.

Gradually, in various ways and through the action of different groups, a tradition of learning developed. Five groups played an important role in its development: the Sanhaja Berbers, the Djula Wangara, the Ineslemen Zawaya, the Fulani and the Shurafa (Hiskett 1985:44 et seq.).

The Sanhaja Berbers

Superficially Islamized up until the eleventh century, the Sanhaja Berbers became rooted in 'Islamic orthodoxy' by adopting the Maliki school of law spread by the Almoravid reform movement led by one of them, ᶜAbdallah b. Yasin, who died in 1059. A deformation of the Arab *al-murabit* (plural *al-murabitun*), which finally acquired the meaning of a Muslim militant or reformer, the derived Almoravid word is *ribat*, which gives the idea of a centre of teaching and propaganda. The Arabs had created a large number of *ribat*, from which they pursued the holy war against the Byzantines and the Berbers (Hiskett 1985:7). During the eleventh century, the Almoravid movement split into two wings: the northern wing which conquered North Africa and part of Andalusia and a southern wing that invaded a large part of the Sahara. The Sanhaja Berbers, who supplied most of the troops of the Almoravid movement, were the principal messengers and teachers of medieval Islam in Africa. Ardent proselytizers, they contributed, also in the post-Almoravid period, to the dissemination of Islam and Maliki jurisprudence in the regions of the Sahara and Western Sudan. Many sources show the intellectual influence of the Sanhaja Berbers in the medieval Saharan towns of Walata, Takedda and Timbuktu. The intellectual development of Timbuktu, and notably the establishment of the Sankoré College, is credited to Sanhaja Berber scholars (Hunwick 1997:7).

The Djula Wangara

Another group that is known for having contributed to the spread of the Arab intellectual tradition is called Wangara in the central Sudan, and Jakhanke in Senegambia (Last 1885:2). Current historians locate Wangaraland in the upper basin of the Senegal and Niger rivers. The first mention of this country in the written sources on the history of West Africa was made by Al-Idrissi in the twelfth century, who described it as an Eldorado (Al-Hajj 1968:1). The Djula, who were mainly trading communities were Islamized before the non-trading groups (Hiskett 1985:45). Among them sprang up literary groups. During the sixteenth century, the decline of the Mali empire, which was torn by dynastic struggles, caused large numbers of the population to move towards the central Sudan. Seeking a more secure way of life, but also inspired by their proselytization and teaching vocation, the Djula Wangara also moved towards the Central Sudan. An anonymous chronicle dated 1650, discovered in Nigeria by the Sudanese historian M. A. al-Hajj, reports the massive entry of Wangara missionaries into Kano in the middle of the seventeenth century. Very soon, the Wangara had made a decisive contribution to the Islamization of Kano. When they arrived in Kano under the leadership of Abdarrahaman Zagaité, the situation of Islam was similar to that of most of the Saharan and Sahelian kingdoms and urban centres: it was only practised by the political and commercial elites who traded with the Arabs.

The Wanghara missionaries succeeded, in spite of strong opposition from the population who were mostly pagan, to have *imams* and *qadis* appointed (Al-Hajj 1968:2). The Wangara also set up an Islamic educational system identical to that practised elsewhere in the Muslim world. The Madabo mosque which was established in Kano in the sixteenth century became a college in the medieval sense of the term, attracting teachers and students from the Central Sudan (Uba Adamu n.d.:3). The Wangara made two major contributions to sub-Saharan Islam. On the one hand, they strove to spread Maliki jurisprudence in the region (following the example of the Sanhaja Berbers), mainly through the teaching of the two fundamental Maliki texts: the *Mukhtasar* of Khalil and the *Risala* of Ibn Abi Zayd al-Qayrawani (see Annexure). On the other hand they introduced the first Sufi influences that were inspired by the Qadiriyya. As Sufism and the Maliki school of law are two fundamental characteristics of Islam in West Africa, the impact of the Wangara on this Islam was far from negligible.

The Zawaya

The contribution of the Zawaya to the spread of Islamic knowledge was also decisive. These tribes, of whom Abdel Weddoud Ould Cheikh (1985:51-59) listed more than a hundred in Mauritania alone, are different from warrior Berber tribes in that they specialized in religious activities and the transmission of knowledge. In the libraries and collections of manuscripts in the region (Kane 1994), there is a large number of works by all kinds of Zawaya authors. Their intellectual influence on the Western Sudan is reflected by the popularity of their Islamic teaching. Many Islamic teaching centres in West Africa call on members of the Zawaya tribes to teach the Koran. The other aspect of their intellectual influence in sub-Saharan Africa is the introduction of Sufism. The Zawaya tribes initiated black Africans to the two dominant Sufi brotherhoods of sub-Saharan Africa, the Tijaniyya and the Qadiriyya. Most chains of transmission of the Tijaniyya can be traced to Muhammad al-Hafiz (1759/60-1830) and his tribe, the Idaw ali, while those of the Qadiriyya go back mostly to the Kunta, another maraboutic tribe whose two most important figures, Shaykh Sidi Mukhtar al-Kunti al-Kabir (1729-1811) and his son Sidi Muhammad (who died in 1826), were the authors of numerous works.

The Fulbe

Known as the Fulani by the Hausa of the Northern Region of Nigeria, Peul by the French and Fellata in Borno and Nilotic Sudan (Hunwick 1997:14), the Fulbe have also played an important role in propagating Islam and spreading literacy in Arabic and *a'jami*. One of the largest linguistic groups in black Africa, they are to be found everywhere in the Sudano-Sahalien belt. They originated from the Senegal River Valley and speak a language belonging to the Niger-Congo group. Between the eleventh and the nineteenth century, they spread throughout the whole West African Savannah (Horton 1985:113). The Fulbe are now present from Senegal to Nilotic Sudan and there is a strong concentration of them in northern Nigeria. Although they converted to Islam after the Wangara, they became no less ardent proselytizers and teachers. As from the fifteenth century, many Fulbe specialized in scholarship, leading movements of religious reform in the western and central Sudan and creating theocratic states.

The Shurafa

The word *Shurafa* is the plural of *sharif*, which means noble in Arabic. In the Islamic tradition, the term refers to the descendants of the Prophet. There are many groups in the Muslim world who claim this title but it has been difficult to authenticate their claims because of the 'principle of genealogical sophistication'. This consists, for the groups having acquired a reputation for knowledge, piety and holiness, of trying to consolidate this reputation by claiming an Arab or *sharifian* descent. Many who make such claims are scholars. However, unlike ulama whose legitimacy rests on the sole knowledge of texts, the legitimacy of *shurafa* is based basically on the assumption that their Sharifian origin gives them supernatural powers to harm their adversaries, to cure the sick, to predict the future and to bestow good luck and happiness on those who venerate them.

These five groups have contributed decisively to the Islamic scholarly tradition in black Africa. The Arabophones, like the Zawaya, have written essentially in Arabic, while the others wrote in Arabic and in *a'jami*.

4

The Development of *d'jami* Literature

The growth of writing in this form has very often been a process by which speakers of vernacular languages, in contact with the written foreign language, appropriated it to transcribe their own language. In Western Europe, Latin was for a long time the language of learning par excellence. Towards the end of the Middle Ages it was relegated to second rank by the European vernacular languages. For example, before 1500, 77 per cent of the books printed in Western Europe were written in Latin (Anderson 1991:18). Then, between 1500 and 1600, aided by the development of printing, particularly in vernacular languages, between 150 and 200 million books were published, the majority in the vernacular, which gradually acquired the status of scholarly languages (Anderson 1991:33-34).

Arabic has been for many of the Islamized peoples the equivalent of Latin for the peoples of Western Europe, *mutatis mutandis*. Learned people in the Islamized world not only learnt Arabic and contributed to Arab intellectual history, but they appropriated the Arabic characters in order to promote their own languages. There is virtually no region which has historically been under Islamic influence that has not adopted the Arabic alphabet for transcribing non-Arabic languages. The languages transcribed in *d'jami* are as varied as some Slavic languages, Spanish, Persian, Turkish, Urdu, Swahili, Hebrew, Berber, Malay, Afrikaans, but also many African languages. As well as the consonants based on Arabic, *d'jami* has, based on altered Arabic letters, created consonants to render sounds that are unknown in classical Arabic.

The research underway on the heritage of the manuscripts shows that the use of *d'jami* has been widespread in sub-Saharan Africa. Many of the manuscripts that could have given us an idea of the intellectual production in *d'jami* have been lost because of the poor state in which they were conserved (Kane 1994; Knappert 1990). Nevertheless, it is possible to find, in languages as diverse as Wolof, Hausa, Fulani, Mande, Songhai and particularly Swahili, writings in *d'jami* that serve not only as the language of correspondence, but also as the language of learning in which treatises and poems were written. However, it is mostly a devotional literature (Knappert 1990:116). Sometimes it is a translation of Arabic writings, for example the Burda[7] which was translated into Fulani by Shaykh Abou Sa'adu (Knappert 1990:116). In central Sudan, there is a considerable literature in a'jami, which dates mainly from the beginning of the eighteenth century. This intellectual tradition, inherited from the Sokoto Caliphate, developed greatly in the nineteenth and twentieth centuries. Thanks to John Hunwick (1995:86-113), there is a reference source for these texts and authors of the nineteenth and twentieth centuries, both in the Arabic language and in the Hausa and Fulani variants of a'jami (Hunwick 1995, 2002).

In his *History of Hausa Islamic Verses*, Hiskett (1975), one of the greatest specialists in the Hausa language, which is spoken by 40 million people, mainly in northern Nigeria and in southern Niger, classifies the themes of the a'jami verse literature into eight categories (Knappert 1990:123-124):

i. Writings about death and resurrection, the interrogations that the dead undergo in the grave, reward and punishment, and the day of judgement. This group of themes is included in the category of *waazi* (preaching) and *zuhudi* (asceticism);

ii. Panegyrics of the Prophet (*madihi an-nabi*) and sometimes praises of other saints;

iii. Didactic explanations regarding the attributes of God and some basic principles of Muslim theology (*tawhidi*);

iv. Writings on the precepts of Islamic law and concerning personal behaviour, particularly prayer, ablutions, successions (*fikihi*);

v. The biography of the Prophet Muhammad and his companions. This literature also recounts the miracles attributed to the Prophet (*sira*):

vi. Chronicles concerning the history of the region (*tarikhi*);

vii. Writings on astrology (*ilmin nujumi*) and the evaluation of auspicious days for undertaking projects (*hisabi*), calculations. There is abundant literature on this subject which shows how popular it is, not only in Nigeria but in West Africa as a whole;

viii. Texts of a political nature and sometimes invocations (this category is essentially secular).

The Fodiawa authors knew Arabic, as well as the Hausa and Fulani variants of a'jami. Their writings in Arabic were aimed at a public that knew classical Arabic, but their writings in Fulani and Hausa targeted a larger audience which had not mastered Arabic. This pedagogical endeavour aimed at explaining notions such as law, theology and the eschatology of Islam to most of the population who were thus informed about the debates going on in Caliphate literary society. As mentioned earlier, the most famous Fodiawa were Uthman Dan Fodio, Abdullahi Dan Fodio, Muhammadu Bello, but above all the daughter of Bello, Nana Asma'u (1793-1864). In a sub-title of the book written about her, Jean Boyd describes Asma'u as a teacher, a poet and an Islamic leader. It should also be added that she was a mother and a wife who, despite the many constraints of these different responsibilities and despite having lived in precarious and insecure conditions, composed an impressive number of writings in Arabic and *djami* (Fulani and Hausa). Her writings cover a broad range of fields, from women in society to women and the cult of possession (*bori*), history, eschatology, politics, theology, the Caliphate and idealism (Boyd 1989:126). Thanks to Boyd and Mack (1997), we now have the originals and translations into English of the complete works of Nana Asma'u (Boyd and Mack 1997), accompanied by critical notes, commentaries and glossaries so that these texts can be seen in their political, historical and literary contexts.

In northern Nigeria, a school has been established based on the work of Hiskett and the researchers whom he trained and who have played an important role in studying Hausa verses. In addition to his above-mentioned *History of Hausa Islamic Verse,* Hiskett is the author of an anthology of political verses that reviews and analyzes six poems that teach us much about political life in northern Nigeria (Hiskett 1977). Among them figure the works of Mudi Sipkin, born in 1930, and founding member of the Northern Elements Progressive Union of Northern Nigeria. Written in the early 1950s, this Hausa poem by Sipkin entitled *Arewa Jumhuriyya kawai* in Hausa (The North can only be a Republic) was in response to a poem entitled *Arewa Jumhuriyya ko mulkiyya* (The North, a Republic or a Monarchy?) by a member of his party, Saad Zungur, who was also inspired by the confrontation between politicians from the north and the south on the future of Nigeria, at the time of the constitutional conference held in Ibadan in 1950 (Hiskett 1977:8).

Another important work proceeding from what one can perhaps call the 'Hiskett school' is that of Abdulkadir Dangambo. In two volumes of almost 800 pages, this thesis was defended at the School of Oriental and African Studies at London University in 1980 and is devoted to *wakokin waazi* (sermons in verse). Like the panegyrics (*wakokin yaboo*) these sermons in verse constitute one of the main literary categories in Hausa. The material discussed in the thesis covers the period from 1800 to 1970 and constitutes a critical study of the form, content, language and style of the poems belonging to the sermon category.

Also from the Hiskett school and worthy of mention is the thesis defended by Abdullahi Bayero Yahaya at the Department of Nigerian Languages and

Culture of Bayero University in 1983. This is dedicated to a Hausa poet called al-Hajj Bello Yahaya who was trained both in English and Arabic and Islamic studies. Inspired by the beggars who recited the poems of Uthman Dan Fodio in Arabic and Hausa, Bello Yahaya composed poems in Hausa on numerous subjects. He wrote political poems in support of the Northern People's Congress, a party dominated by northern Nigeria in the 1950s and 1960s (Yahaya 1983:7). The sociological and psychological impact of the economic and technological transformations during the colonial period reflected in these poems makes fascinating reading. His poem *Wakar Reluwe* (Song of the Railway) is constructed on the Arab metre *mutaqarab* and opens as follows:

> *Ina gode Allahu mai yau da gobe*
> [Praise be to God to whom today and tomorrow belong]

> *Das sanya Hausa cikin reluwe*
> [For including the Hausa among the users of the train]

Technological progress, far from shaking people's faith, has reinforced it insofar as they first consider that this progress is a blessing that God has bestowed upon them. Al-hajj Bello Yahaya is also the author of many poems about the transformation of social relationships in the colonial era and the emergence of waged labour, as well as praise for the Prophet Muhammad and sermons in verse. Apart from the metre inspired from Arabic metrics, the style of Bello's poems places his work in the Islamic library.

In addition to the development of *ajami* which is an evidence of African agency, there are other types of knowledge inspired by Arabic and Islamic influence in black Africa. Among these forms of knowledge is an exoteric component which links African Islam to the scholarly tradition of classical Islam, as well as an esoteric component that situates this Islam in the everyday concerns of the population, including those who are not Muslim.

5

Esoteric Knowledge and Exoteric Knowledge

Based on a teaching model that started in Mamluk Egypt (Hiskett 1985:16-17), and spread throughout the Muslim world, a two-tier system of Islamic education was set up in Muslim Africa to promote the expansion of Islam. At the lower level, there are the Koranic schools (*kuttab*, plural *katatib* in Arabic) and at the higher level, the science schools (*madrasa*, plural *madaris*). The names of these schools in African languages vary, but their pedagogy and core curriculum tended to be identical throughout the Sudano-Sahelian region, if not in the Muslim world as a whole.

At the Koranic schools, pupils are admitted very young, between four and seven years of age. They are taught how to read and write in the Arabic script before starting to memorize the Koran. Some pupils are able to memorize the whole Koran within three to four years. Others take longer, some never manage it. They are also taught the rudiments of religious practice (ablution, prayer, fasting, etc.). Because parents do not always pay for the tuition and maintenance of their children, and teaching is the main activity of Koranic masters, pupils contribute to the costs of their education either by working in the fields in a rural milieu, or by begging. These days, many urban citizens consider begging as degrading and they criticize the Koranic school teachers whom they hold responsible for an inhuman system of exploitation. However, in their original context, begging was not at all degrading. Those who give have once been those who held out the bowl when they were pupils. Those who receive consider this begging stage of their life as a natural, transitory period that all children have to experience and which prepares them for adult life.

Pupils learn reading and writing at the same time. The learning tool is a wooden tablet. Once or twice a day they copied out on the tablet that part of the Koran they have been assigned to memorize, using black ink made from the charcoal they could scrape off their saucepans at home. After having memorized its contents, they washed their tablets and put them out in the sun to dry so that they could use them again. Wednesday afternoon, all Thursday and Friday morning are holidays for the youngest pupils, while the older ones use these days to go over their past lessons. After they have written and memorized the whole Koran bit by bit (between one and two dozen lines daily), they revise it by reciting larger blocks of texts (several pages at a time) until they are able to recite it all. They then recite the whole Koran in front of a jury made up of *Huffaz* (singular, *hafiz*), people who have memorized the whole book. A successful pupil is known as *hafiz*. Pupils can be asked to recopy a whole manuscript of the Koran in calligraphic characters to see if they can master both the memorizing and the writing. This level of Islamic education applies to a large part of the child population. Whether Muslims are town-dwellers or rural people, it is rare that they have not attended a Koranic school and memorized a certain number of verses, even if it is only to be able to say their daily prayers.

The second level of traditional Islamic education takes place in the *madaris*, to which are admitted pupils who have memorized all or a large part of the Koran. While the children at the *katatib* only have to memorize what they are reading, without understanding it, at the *madaris* they follow advanced courses enabling them to understand Arabic, and to express themselves in that language. These schools are of unequal quality. Some, inherited from the medieval colleges, provide a complete course so that their graduates are recognized as *ulama*. Others offer a more restricted curriculum. Thus, the keener students spend a long time, going from one master to another so as to deepen their knowledge in a given discipline.

Among the schools that give a complete training, the college of Pire Saniokhor in Senegal is a good example. Thanks to Thierno Kâ, we have a wealth of information on this college which was based on the town of Pire, halfway between Dakar and Saint Louis and which was attended by many scholars (Kâ 1982). The training was essentially oral. The teacher taught all the books, chapter by chapter, reading them first in Arabic and then translating them in African languages. A student capable of reading in Arabic and translating the contents of a given book into an African language was assumed to have mastered it and given an *ijaza* (authorization to transmit knowledge) by his teacher. Some students study the same book several times before mastering it. This traditional education tends to be very scholastic.

In certain regions of Africa, there are scholars who specialized in teaching how to memorize the Koran. In Hausaland and Borno, they are called *alarama* (plural *alaramomi*) (Kane 2003: chapter 2). They have memorized the Koran and know how many times rare words occur, but do not necessarily understand the meaning of the verses. They are also very skilled in the widespread art in Africa of fabricating talismans, philtres and charms based on the Koran.

Apart from the knowledge dispensed by Islamic schools, which could be described as exoteric, there were also other types of knowledge which, as they are spelt out in texts, made a major contribution to the development of Islam in sub-Saharan Africa. This knowledge was mainly expressed through a magical usage of the Koran and it enabled Muslim scholars to respond to the demand of a clientele that was looking for happiness, a cure, prosperity, fecundity and protection against enemies (both real and imaginary). Since the pre-colonial period, during which African sovereigns would request talismans from the marabouts, up to the present day, the clientele of these marabouts has not diminished, however much the modernization theories might deplore it. Often a person who is looking for, loses or fears to lose a job will consult a marabout. The same goes for someone who has embezzled funds and is afraid of being arrested. Sick people who do not have the means of getting hospital treatment, as well as those whom modern medicine does not succeed in curing, will go to a marabout. Whatever the level of knowledge or status, the clientele will follow the marabout's recommendations. They will wear talismans, sacrifice sheep, cattle or goats, or wash themselves with philtres, if necessary. In the political field, the marabouts are very often consulted. There are few politicians who have not consulted one or several of them. These marabouts are responsible for protecting them from spells cast by their adversaries or for destroying them – if not for influencing the outcome of elections by supernatural forces.

The works of Louis Brenner and Constant Hames provide invaluable information on this esoteric knowledge. Brenner (1985) analyzed geomancy and the central role it plays in West African societies (see his chapter iv) and he argues that, in spite of the condemnations of the *ulama*, who preach a very legalistic version of Islam, geomancy nevertheless responds to the expectations of the majority of the population. In his analysis of the Kabbe, an Islamic theological teaching in Fulfulde inspired by the *Umm al-barahin* (source of proofs) of Al-Sanusi, Brenner (1985) shows the ability of West African Muslims to appropriate the Islamic heritage and adapt it to their own milieu. This minimal theological teaching attracted women as well as those for whom a more in-depth approach would be more difficult to access (Brenner 1985:63).

Hames's work (1987, 1993, 1997a, 1997b) has shown that in spite of this belief being widespread, the concept of magic derived from the Koran and its materialization through the use of talismans is not only held by the illiterate Muslim masses. It is to be found in the sources of Islamic orthodoxy. Not only did authors like Ibn Qayyim Al-Jawziyya (1292-1350) make unambiguous statements about the orthodoxy of the talismanic usage of the Koran (Hames 1997b:139 et seq.), but also the most reliable compilers of traditions, particularly Muslim and Bukhari, have reported undisputedly authentic accounts that legitimize the talismanic use of the Koran (Hames 1997b:139 et seq.).

The role of the magic Koran in Islamic theology is not well-known for two reasons. The first is that the Orientalists, who were heirs of the Enlightenment, with their desire to apprehend Islam 'rationally', failed to study the magical uses of the Koran, leaving this to the heresiologists and the anthropologists. Hames (1997b:139 et seq.) states that in the entry for Ibn Qayyim Al-Jawziyya in the second edition of the *Encyclopaedia of Islam*, there is no mention of the book *al-tibb al-nabawi* (Prophetic medicine) by this author, which is mainly concerned with the talismanic aspect of the Koran.

The second reason for the lack of recognition of the orthodoxy of the talismanic use of the Koran is that classical authors like Ibn Taymiyya and Ibn Qayyim Al-Jawziyya, who are considered by a certain literature to be the inspiration of the most rigorous fundamentalist movements like the Wahhabis, are often read according to the interpretation that the latter give to their work. The Wahhabis, in their war against the Sufi brotherhoods and the cult of saints, have rejected outright everything that could be used to legitimize them, including the talismanic use of the Koran (Hames 1997b:141 et seq.).

Having briefly surveyed the transmission networks of Islamic knowledge, I will now address the ways in which this knowledge inspired Muslim scholars to speak out politically before European colonization took place.

6

Political/Intellectual Revolutions

During the pre-colonial period, jihads had led to the creation of theocratic states in different parts of West Africa. These jihads had certain common denominators. For one thing, they were started by learned scholars. So profoundly were they influenced by this tradition that they were frustrated by the syncretism that affected Islamic practice. They wanted to establish a political system that corresponded with the prophetic ideal that they had read about in the Islamic manuals that circulated in the region. They saw their efforts as being in the tradition of the struggle for the purification of Islam that went back to the Almoravid movement of the eleventh century, the objectives of which were to apply Maliki Islam in all its rigour. In the writings of these intellectuals, as well as in their sermons and propaganda, one can detect a language of political contestation expressed in Islamic terms. Such language, when it echoes aspirations for emancipation, can mobilize large sectors of the population.

Among the mobilizing concepts for political action is the obligation to command the good and forbid the evil (*al-amr bi 'l-ma'ruf wa al-nahy an al-munkar*). If the role of proselytization in the public sphere of Muslim countries is to be understood, it is crucial to grasp the powerful effect of the language of political contestation. It is not enough for the good Muslim just to practise the five pillars of Islam: belief in God and in the Prophet Muhammad, carrying out the five canonical prayers, fasting during the month of Ramadan and performing the pilgrimage to Mecca. It is also necessary to uphold the good and avoid the evil. The notions of good and evil apply to all that Islam allows and all that it prohibits. How to do this varies according to the groups. Before the eighteenth century, there were two different views among the Muslim scholars. There were those who were inspired by the teachings of Al-Suyuti, and who were engaged in trade. They were pacifists, trying through their behaviour to provide a model of how Islam should be followed in order to lead the population towards more orthodox Islamic practice. Maraboutic tribes like the Kunta and communities like the Jakhanke held such views.

Then there were scholars who were inspired by the thinking of Al-Maghili, who were quicker to take up arms against their opponents (Last 1985:1-2). Both groups developed especially in the urban centres and lived from trade, while trying to purify Islam within the limits of their means.

During the eighteenth century, the crisis of the pastoral economy brought about the re-conversion of many Fulani to scholarship. Thus, the number of scholars increased considerably. The new class of scholars were essentially rural people. They tended to consider urban scholars as corrupt. Many scholars preferred to live in the countryside, far from those 'urban places of perdition', in order to organize their community in conformity with the laws of Islam. Others toured round the neighbouring regions to preach a purer Islam (Last 1985:4-5). Among the many intellectuals who, through their writings and their action, had a lasting impact on West Africa are the Fulani who led the jihads of the nineteenth century, like Karamokho Alpha in Fouta Djallon, Suleyman Baal in Fouta Toro, Uthman Dan Fodio in northern Nigeria, Ahmad Lobbo in Macina, and Al-Hajj Omar at Ségou.

Belief in the imminence of the end of the world and the arrival of the *mahdi* (an eschatological figure in Islamic millenarianism) strengthened the ability of jihad leaders to mobilize the people around them. While not all of them proclaimed themselves mahdi, they utilized these beliefs in order to mobilize or stimulate their troops. The most celebrated of these movements took place in the Sudan. Led by Muhammad Ahmad, who proclaimed himself mahdi in the Nilotic Sudan, this mahdist movement challenged the British army, killed the British General Gordon and established an Islamic state that lasted for several years before being completely defeated in January 1900, when the last emir of the mahdist state was captured (Prunier 1998:41).

In West Africa, the belief in the coming end of the world and the arrival of the mahdi helped jihad leaders to mobilize people for jihads. Among those carried out in the pre-colonial era and at the beginning of the colonial invasion, we shall cite five, before assessing their impact on the Islamic scholarly tradition.

It was under the leadership of Karamokho Alpha that Muslim scholars, supported by traders and pastoralists, led the first jihad of the eighteenth century (1727-1728) in Fouta Djallon. It was directed against the Jalonke who were overcome by the victorious jihadists. The state that resulted was known as the Imamate of Fouta Djallon. In half a century, the Imamate succeeded in changing the decentralized Mande society conquered by the jihadists into a federation governed by Islamic law, with mosques and a network of schools (Last 1985:9). It was in this Imamate, which subsequently inspired similar movements of state building, that Fulani poems began to be composed which were to spread throughout the western and central Sudan (Last 1985:10).

The second jihad of the eighteenth century took place in Fouta Toro. Led by Suleyman Baal, this jihad waged by Muslim scholars of various social origins who called themselves *torodbe*, succeeded in chasing the Moors and the Denyankobbe out of central Fouta in 1760 and 1770 (Last 1985:13). Suleyman Baal was assassinated in 1776 and the movement was then led by Abd al-Qadir Kane. This second Imamate consisted of a federation of villages headed by scholars who were responsible for providing Islamic education and for the administration of justice. It was a considerable step forward in spreading the Islamic scholarly tradition.

The jihad led by Uthman Dan Fodio in Hausaland in the nineteenth century was similar to the eighteenth century jihads. Dan Fodio was the author of various writings and sermons in Arabic, Hausa and Fulfulde. His most important work (Last 1967:9) is entitled *Ihya al-sunna wa ikhmad al-bid'a* (Reviving the tradition of the Prophet Muhammad and destroying innovation).[8] This is another formulation of the precept to command the good and forbid evil. It inspired the struggle against the Hausa kingdoms, mobilizing the different peoples who were being oppressed by them. These were the pastoralists, mainly Fulani, and the farmers who were severely taxed to sustain the lifestyle of the pre-colonial Hausa aristocracy. Hence, the jihad of the nineteenth century in Hausaland has been interpreted as a socioeconomic rebellion, an ethnic revolt, and a pastoral revolution. However, given the core role of the Islamic ideal in the mobilization for this jihad and the society that the jihadists strove to establish, the movement led by Uthman Dan Fodio has also been interpreted as a movement for religious reform.

A fourth jihad, which led to an aristocracy of knowledge coming into power in West Africa in the nineteenth century, was the one in Macina. This jihad, led by Ahmad Lobbo, was to some extent an extension of the jihad of Uthman Dan Fodio. Lobbo and his disciples, who then claimed total independence from Sokoto, were not very erudite, but very pious. Lobbo mobilized his Fulani compatriots, preaching an egalitarian Muslim society to the oppressed (Last 1985:33). After the battle of Noukouma of 1818 against a coalition made up of Ardoen Fulanis and their overlords (the Diarra dynasty of Ségou), a Muslim state was created in Macina. The state took the name of Dina and Ahmad Lobbo became its Caliph, and established its capital at Hamdallahi (Last 1985:32). The supreme body of the Dina was a council of 40 members headed by a learned scholar (Hiskett 1985:178). Like earlier ones, this jihad also contributed to spreading Islamic sciences and the Arabic language. After the death of Ahmad Lobbo in 1845, numerous factions developed in his family in the struggle to control power and this weakened the regime, alienating many of the Muslim scholars from Macina in the process. Some of them rallied Al-Hajj Omar Tall, who conquered Macina in 1859 and integrated it into his empire which had resulted from a fifth jihad with important repercussions in the Western Sudan.

A towering figure of African Islam, Al-Hajj Omar Tall was born at Halwar a 1794 and died in 1864 on the cliffs of Bandiagara. He differed greatly from many of the Muslim scholars of his time as he had travelled widely. In 1825, he made the pilgrimage to Mecca where he studied for three years. With a disciple of Shaykh Ahmad al-Tijani called Muhammad al-Ghali, Omar deepened his knowledge of the Tijaniyya to which he had been initiated in his home country. Muhammad Ghali appointed al-Hajj Omar as the representative (khalifa) of the Tijaniyya in sub-Saharan Africa. Omar then produced his magnum opus *Rimah hizb al-rahim ala nuhur hizb al-rajim* (The spears of the party of the merciful against the throat of the party of the damned). He put forward the dogmas of the new Sufi order of which he became one of the main exponents and the spearhead in sub-Saharan Africa. Like the Jawahir al-maʿani (Jewels of meanings) dictated by Ahmad al-Tijani to his disciple Ali Harazim, on the margins of which the *Rimah* is reproduced, the latter constitutes one of the main doctrinal sources of the Tijaniyya, which counts tens of millions among its followers in the world, most of whom live in sub-Saharan Africa. Unlike the Qadiriyya that had preceded it, the Tijaniyya very soon proved to be a brotherhood open to all – young people, women, and so on.

When he stayed in Sokoto, Al-Hajj was the guest of Caliph Muhammad Bello, who gave him his daughter in marriage. Inspired by his experience in Sokoto, Omar led a holy war against Ségou in 1852, which ended in the construction of a huge empire centred on Ségou (Robinson 1988 *passim*). A scholar as well as a warrior, al-Hajj Omar was, as previously mentioned, a towering figure of West African Islam.

These five jihads are far from being the only ones. There were many others in the western and central Sudan that were inspired by Islam. To the extent that these jihads were led by scholars who toppled illiterate rulers to set up political systems that corresponded to an Islamic ideal, these jihads were as much military revolutions as intellectual revolutions (Hiskett 1985). It is true that they did not succeed in instituting a 'purified Islam' everywhere: the practices and beliefs denounced by the jihadists were not always eradicated. However, they led to an unprecedented growth of the Islamic scholarly tradition. Of course, before the expansion of Islam in Africa, graphic systems of representation had circulated among some populations. This was the case, for example with the alphabet *tfinagah* of Saharan Berbers used as far in the Niger Bend (Hiskett 1985:242). But there had been no scholarly tradition in sub-Saharan Africa that paralleled the Islamic one.

The dissemination of knowledge, as we have shown, did not only consist in the emergence of an Arabized clergy, but also in the growth of an erudite literature in the form of *djami* poetry. The impact of these jihads on the intellectual life in West Africa was very great. It brought about an unprecedented spread of centres of learning. In addition, it paved the way for the rise of typically Muslim cities with Islamic institutions, thus rooting an Arabic-*djami* intellectual tradition which was, however, to undergo some transformations after the colonial conquest.

7

European Colonization and the Transformation of Islamic Education

The second half of the nineteenth century was a turning point in the history of Africa and that of Islam in Africa, as well as that of the Islamic scholarly tradition. Europeans had been present in the region for three centuries but they had been limited to the coastal areas. In 1880, they hardly occupied more than a tenth of the total landmass of the continent. Two decades later, all Africa had been conquered, except for Ethiopia, Liberia and Morocco – and this last was occupied in 1912. The pre-colonial African states (both Islamized and not) were all overcome by the military supremacy of the Westerners.

The interpretations of colonization inspired by the colonial library presented the European imperial project as consistent, emphasizing the notion that it was conceived to liberate the colonized peoples from the traditions in which they were imprisoned and to lead them towards modernity. This kind of interpretation has been challenged by an abundant literature produced in the former colonies after their independence. Described as post-colonial studies, this literature has challenged numerous assumptions about modernity and European imperialism.

According to certain thinkers of the post-colonial school, the construction of modernity did not originate in the West from whence it was to be exported to the rest of the world by the Westerners. It was the culmination of a period of intense interaction and strong interconnections between the West and the rest of the world, which was therefore a partner in the construction of modernity (Chakrabarty 1999:104). The corollary was that the colonial state was not a monolithic entity, but was composed of individuals and forces that sometimes diverged in their approach and were often carried out on an ad hoc basis. When the state did not dispose of the necessary human and material resources to implement its policy, it was often changed, in response to the agency of colonized people.

This brings us to another fundamental assumption of the post-colonial school, that of the capacity of the dominated to influence a relationship of domination. The colonized were not passive subjects, but political actors. Their agency sometimes went in the opposite direction to that desired by the Europeans, who lacked the means of opposing them. Action by the colonized could even make the colonial state change its initial project. The different usages of Islam by the colonized peoples of sub-Saharan Africa in the colonial period show the resources possessed by the 'subaltern in a subordination situation'. In addition, there were mahdist movements, which formed part of a deeply rooted tradition and which tried to struggle against the colonial order and subvert it through violence. These movements were often repressed. But there were other, much more subtle ones that negotiated forms of compromise with the colonizer while continuing to pursue their own objectives. This was the orientation of the political establishment of the marabouts who, in French West Africa, succeeded in imposing themselves as the principal partners of the colonial state. A good illustration was the Muslim Societies in West Africa project, under colonial domination, which organized two international conferences and published two reference works on the question (Robinson and Triaud 1997; Triaud and Robinson 2000). It showed how the maraboutic political establishment in French West Africa was able to take advantage of the opportunities provided by colonial peace to consolidate its economic, social and intellectual base. Not only did the marabouts continue to proselytize on behalf of Islam and their brotherhood, they also intensified their efforts to promote the Arabic language.

The educational system established by the colonial state and the missionaries, the chief purveyors of modern education, promoted European languages to the detriment of Arabic after the conquest of Africa. Writing in African languages was encouraged in certain regions, but Latin characters were preferred to the Arabic ones, so that the two systems of transcribing African languages co-existed: one in the Arabic script mainly used by non-Europhone readers and the other in the Latin script. The growth of literacy in Western languages and the use of the Latin script did not cause a decline of the Islamic scholarly tradition, but its transformation and the diversification of the networks for training Muslim scholars. These transformations, without eliminating the initial system, promoted the emergence of new categories of Arabists. These were the graduates of modernized Arabic teaching and those trained in universities and other institutions of higher learning in the Arab-Islamic world. Like their predecessors, these Arabists were to take part in politics. The sections that follow analyze the transformations of the Islamic educational system, the emergence of these intellectuals and their political discourse.

8

Modernization of the Islamic
Educational System

After the colonial conquest of Africa, Muslim populations were reluctant to attend secular schools. Given the need for sufficiently qualified staff to run the administration, the colonial state created modernized Arab-Islamic schools. Such was the case of the French *medersa* of Timbuktu. However, as Brenner (1997:471) has correctly observed, the creation of medersa in West Africa aimed less at promoting Islamic education than at changing it to undermine the influence of the maraboutic establishment. The curriculum of medersa included some elements of French culture in an educational system that was basically religious. Therefore it was different from the educational system that was entirely in English, French or Portuguese, according to the colonies, which trained the political and administrative elite who inherited the African states at the end of the colonial reign.

Some Muslims, realizing the limits of the traditional Islamic teaching, strove to modernize it, by drawing inspiration from the system set up by the colonial administration. To do this, they diversified the educational curriculum by introducing other subject matter and creating different levels of teaching, corresponding to the age of the students. The pedagogical materials also underwent a transformation. The teaching that had been essentially oral became partly written. Teachers used a blackboard and chalk to write and the pupils abandoned their wooden tablets in favour of exercise books and pens. In many cases, private initiatives for modernizing the traditional Islamic teaching were interpreted as political acts and opposed (Brenner 1997:491). This was the case of the medersa created by Saada Umar Touré at Ségou (Mali) which ultimately served as the model for renovating the Islamic teaching that used Arabic as the language of learning. The French colonial administration blocked all the initiatives to create other schools along the lines of the medersa of Saada Omar Touré. In the same vein, it supported initiatives aimed at promoting a system of Islamic education using African languages, particularly Bambara and Fulani (Brenner 1997:487).

The experience of the modernized Islamic schools in Northern Nigeria was very similar. The colonial state created a few modern Arab-Islamic schools to train administrative staff. One of the most famous was the School of Arabic Studies at Kano. Muslims products of this modern educational system used it to set up networks of formal Arab-Islamic schools as, for instance, was done by Aminu Kano (who died in 1983). In the 1950s, he developed a system of modern Islamic schools under the name of Islamiyya schools. Very quickly, the system met with success, for not only did the pupils assimilate the Koran more rapidly, they also learnt Arabic relatively easily while they were still young. Soon, numerous schools of the same kind were created in other towns of Nigeria (Bray 1981:59-60). Nevertheless, because Aminu Kano was the leader of the Northern Elements Progressive Union (NEPU), a party that opposed the Northern People's Congress (NPC) that governed the region, the NPC sent thugs to destroy these schools and, out of a total of sixty, only three survived.

It was, above all, in the post-colonial period that the modernized Islamic schools experienced considerable growth. Northern Nigeria is undoubtedly where this growth in the new Arab-Islamic schools has been most prodigious. A major motivation was to ensure that formal education in northern Nigeria caught up with that of the south. This was partly due to the indirect rule policy that prohibited the Christian missions, who were mainly responsible for modern schools, from setting up and preaching in certain Muslim areas. With the ascension of Nigeria to independence, it was essential for the northerners to overcome this deficiency and, on the initiative of Ahmadu Bello, real efforts were made to modernize the Koranic schools. They received subsidies for the construction of classrooms and employment of teachers who could give a general education. The Hausa language, transcribed in the Latin script, a development encouraged by the British during the colonial period through the publication of books and journals, also underwent considerable development. Hausa now has the status of an official Nigerian language, in contrast with the situation in most of the West African countries, where only very timid initiatives have been taken to develop their national languages. There exists an abundant literature as well as daily newspapers and journals in the Hausa language. Many intellectuals hold lectures and write academic papers in Hausa.

Thanks to the oil revenue, however, formal education was to develop even more remarkably in Nigeria in the 1970s. There is no field in which the oil manna has not had some positive effect. As far as primary education is concerned, the Universal Primary Education programme was adopted in 1977. One year after the programme was launched, the official number of children in primary school was 9.5 million – more than the entire population of any other single West African country (Bray 1981:1). Even if the federated states blew up their figures to attract maximum funding from the federal state, which was the chief provider of finance at that time, there is no doubt that primary education experienced tremendous growth. It was the same story for secondary and higher education. The latter was even more remarkable: with two universities at independence and five at the beginning of the oil boom, Nigeria has in 2011 over a hundred universities.

Oil revenue has also affected the number of modern Islamic schools. Apart from the resources that Nigeria injected into them, Muslim oil-producing countries in the Persian Gulf have contributed to financing modernized Arab-Islamic education (Kane 2003:chapter 2). Funding, didactic materials and teachers were sent to Nigeria by certain organizations in the Arab countries of the Gulf, particularly Saudi Arabia, as part of their pan-Islamic policy. Although Nigeria received a large part of Saudi assistance, it was not the only country to do so. Numerous countries of Africa and Asia, as well as Muslim communities in the West benefited from the largesse of oil countries desiring to promote Arab-Islamic education (Kepel 2000:69 et seq.). The reform of Islamic teaching affected mainly primary and secondary schooling.

In Senegal, the reform of Arabic teaching took place in various fields. First, numerous colleges for teaching Arabic were established. These colleges, like the Ma'had Shaykh Abdullah Niasse of Kaolack, the Dar al-Quran of Dakar and the Manar al-Huda Institute of Louga, train Arabists until they obtain their secondary school certificates. Collaboration with Arab countries and institutions, the Al-Azhar University in Cairo in particular, provides technical assistance in the form of teachers to the above institutions and hundreds of others of the same kind in Africa. The certificates awarded by these schools are recognized by Al-Azhar and enable students, on completing their secondary education, to continue more advanced studies at the Egyptian university.

Another dimension of the reform of Arabic teaching was the creation of the so-called French-Arabic schools. Some of these were established by post-colonial governments concerned with harmonizing the teaching and creating outlets for the graduates of the local Arabic schools. Others have been set up by religious personalities or graduates from universities of the Arab world. These French-Arabic schools admit pupils who have already attended the Koranic schools and have memorized the Koran either totally or partially. In contrast with the traditional schools, the French-Arabic ones offer general education in Arabic, with courses in the French language at an elementary level. They award certificates that are recognized by the state and their graduates can apply for a job, very often as teachers or professors in colleges teaching Arabic. Some of the graduates of French-Arabic schools continue their studies in Arab countries and, more rarely, in African universities. In spite of the efforts made to provide them with jobs, the Arabists have greater difficulties than their counterparts trained in Western or African universities, in European languages, to obtain salaried posts.

In sub-Saharan Africa, there are two institutions of higher learning where teaching is essentially in Arabic, one in Niger and one in Uganda. The idea of creating one in Niger dates back to the summits of the kings and heads of states of Muslim sovereigns countries and presidents of Muslim nations held in Lahore in 1974 (Triaud 1988:160). But the project did not get underway until 1982 when construction work began on the Faculty of Islamic Studies and Arabic Language. Created for students from Francophone countries, the Islamic University is based at Say, beside the River Niger, and it will also include faculties of science, medicine, economics, etc. It has the following objectives:

i.   To consolidate an Islamic identity through the study of the Islamic and Arabic heritage and to enrich the life of Muslims in Africa by integrating the foundations of its civilization and putting them at the service of society;

ii. To enable students to have access to science and technology and to apply the scientific knowledge acquired in the service of the well-being of Muslim peoples and countries;

iii. To establish academic research and study of social problems in light of Islamic thinking, integrated into the needs of the milieu within the framework of Islamic cooperation;

iv. To create a movement of activities and the orientation of publications of the Islamic heritage in the African continent, encouraging research and efforts seeking an understanding of Islam;

v.   To train competent staff and provide the necessary means for teaching and for advanced studies in different fields of knowledge and science;

vi. To pay special attention to Arabic and Islamic studies; and

vii. To provide cultural, sporting and scientific activities (Triaud 1988:160-61).

In West Africa, the Islamic University of Niger is the most advanced local initiative seeking to offer high quality training to local Arabists. It also aims to make known the Arab-Islamic cultural tradition.

The Islamic University of Uganda, which was founded by the Organization of the Islamic Conference in 1988, is aimed at nationals of the Anglophone countries south of the Sahara (Useen 1999 *passim*). The teaching is in Arabic and English. In 1999, it had some 1,100 students, divided into four faculties or high schools: literature and social sciences, educational sciences, management and Islamic heritage. It plans to increase its buildings to accommodate a student population of 10,000 in the near future and to increase the percentage of recruitment of its female students from 30 to 50. In some disciplines, an Islamic perspective is taught through complementary courses. As well as the economics traditionally taught in faculties of economics, students in these courses receive specific teaching on the Islamic principles on interest, taxes and insurance. The university also includes among its teaching staff some Christians. The non-Muslim female students have to conform to the normal Muslim standards on dress and must cover their heads (Useen 1999).

Like these two universities, the higher education of most African Arabists took place — and still does — in the universities of the Arab world.

9

Sub-Saharan African Arabists and Higher Education in the Arab World

The theocratic Muslim states of the nineteenth century, from the Umarian state of Ségou to the Mahdist state of Sudan, not forgetting the Sokoto Caliphate in Northern Nigeria, were fiercely opposed to European colonization. Hence, following the consolidation of European colonial rule, the British and the French, who took the lion's share in the division of Africa, set up a quarantine line between North Africa and sub-Saharan Africa, in order to avoid Islam becoming a base for a 'subversive' mobilization of colonial subjects. Independence from colonial domination then became an opportunity for cooperation and the renewal of ties between the North African countries and the Islamized countries south of the Sahara. In this context, the Arab countries offered many scholarships to African students, both through the official channels of diplomacy and through African Muslim personalities who distributed them to their constituencies. Thanks to these scholarships, students trained in the Koranic and traditional Arab-Islamic schools had an opportunity to continue their secondary studies and higher education in Arab countries.

The training of sub-Saharan African Arabists in the Arab world is a field for research that has long been neglected. Most of the work on sub-Saharan Islam has focused on Sufi orders. In rare cases, they mention without going into detail, the involvement of Arabists in political contestation when they return to their countries. The first substantial work was carried out by a group of researchers in the Centre d'étude d'Afrique noire in Bordeaux (Otayek 1992).[9] Thanks to their work, we now have better information on certain networks for training Arabists. Egypt, Morocco, Saudi Arabia, Tunisia, Libya and Sudan are the main Arab countries receiving sub-Saharan African Arabists.

For a long time, Egypt was preferred by Arabists from sub-Saharan Africa and thousands of them have trained there (Mattes 1993:50). At the beginning of the 1960s, eighty-two Senegalese students were attending Al-Azhar University, together with hundreds of nationals of other West African countries. At the time, the Al-Azhar University served as a policy instrument for Egyptian President Gamal Abdel Nasser, who saw himself as a leader of the Third World. The Egyptian president tried to mobilize as much support as possible in the Muslim world and in the Third World in general, which is why Al-Azhar received so many African students. After Nasser's death, Al-Azhar continued to be an instrument for Egypt's cultural policy and welcomed thousands of students from the Muslim world. It also supplied technical assistance, especially teachers, to most of the Arabic schools and institutions of learning in sub-Saharan Africa.

Until the 1990s, most of the schools teaching Arabic in sub-Saharan Africa provided no secondary schooling. Thus, the graduates of these schools going to Al-Azhar did not tackle university level studies immediately, but followed remedial courses in a specialized institute at Al-Azhar for non-Arabophone students. After a few years of study, the African Arabists were admitted to the faculties of the Al-Azhar University. A very small number of them were admitted in Egyptian high schools. After completing high school, this minority was then qualified to study scientific subjects at Al-Azhar or other Egyptian institutions like Cairo University and the ʿAyn Al-Shams University. Most African students were in the faculties of religious studies. Upon their return to Africa, they suffered from a double handicap. The first was that they have received instruction in a language other than that of the administration or of the business world. The second was that their expertise was not highly valued in the job market. Thus, competition with graduates from the schools of engineering, business and even literature who trained in the Europhone universities of Africa or Europe, found them at a disadvantage.

This unfortunate experience of the first generation trained at Al-Azhar and in other Arabic countries, and who found difficulty in securing employment back home, had an impact on the second generation. Some of the second generation, rather than return to their country after graduating from Arab universities, left for Europe. France was the favourite destination for citizens of former French colonies because the French universities had established equivalence systems that enabled nationals from Arab countries to be admitted. A number of African graduates from Arab universities took advantage of this system to pursue graduate studies in France. Some humanities students attended the National Institute of Oriental Languages and Civilizations in Paris. However, most of the Arabist Africans who were admitted to universities could not succeed in exams because of poor command of French. Those who were admitted for postgraduate studies were luckier, for they obtained their doctorates without having a good knowledge of French. As they did not intend to work in France (at least it was assumed), their dissertation sponsors were not too demanding regarding their command of the French language. However, upon their return to their country of origin (such as Chad, Cameroon, Senegal, Mali, Niger), these Arabists who possessed a French degree had better chances of obtaining professional occupations than their peers who spoke only Arabic.

Morocco was one of the first countries to welcome African Arabists. Like Egypt, Morocco's policy aimed at extending its zone of influence to the Muslim countries of West Africa. It should be noted that sub-Saharan Islam, which is dominated by Sufi orders, is strongly influenced by Moroccan Islam. In fact, the Sufi order that was most widespread in sub-Saharan Africa, the Tijaniyya, was an Algerian-Moroccan brotherhood (Triaud and Robinson 2000: *passim*). Following its spread, there were cultural ties between the different *tijani* communities of sub-Saharan Africa and Morocco. At the beginning of the 1960s, Morocco, in the name of its historical presence in part of the sub-Saharan territory, claimed a Great Morocco that extended to the north of Senegal. The cultural ties that existed between Morocco and Africa south of the Sahara, as well as the political ambitions of King Hassan II, constitute the background of Moroccan policy towards sub-Saharan Africa, which is expressed not only in the formal channels of diplomacy but also in the informal sector of international relations. King Hassan II had special ties with the Muslims of sub-Saharan Africa, particularly with the leaders of the Sufi brotherhoods. Through the influence of the latter, scholarships were given to Arabists from West Africa to study in Morocco as from the early 1960s and, to date, Morocco continues to receive nationals from the Muslim countries of sub-Saharan Africa.

African students were studying in Algeria before it obtained independence. Some of the first Senegalese Muslim reformers were trained in that country. Cheikh Touré, the former leader of the Muslim Cultural Union, and Alioune Diouf, the first emir of the Ibadou Rahman movement, studied in Algeria during the 1950s (Loimeier 1994:57). After Algerian independence and, above all, after the oil boom, thousands of scholarships were offered to African students by Algeria (Mattes 1993:50). Some of them were trained in the humanities and religious studies in Arabic, others in scientific disciplines in Arabic and in French.

Libya, under Colonel Ghadaffi, was also one of the Arab countries that welcomed students from black Africa. When Ghadaffi came to power, two institutions were created to promote Libya's cultural policy: the Association for the Islamic Appeal (*Jam῾iyyat al-da῾wa al-islamiyya*), founded in 1972, and the Faculty for the Islamic Appeal (*Kuliyyat al da῾wa al-islamiyya* – AAI), set up in 1974. The latter has branches in Syria, Lebanon, Pakistan and England (Mattes 1993:43) and offers various university degrees, culminating in a doctorate (Mattes 1993:44). An excellent propaganda machine, the AAI is well-financed and has considerable freedom in transferring funds abroad. It is active in a number of fields, including preaching and training, communication and financial support (Mattes 1993:42-43), and has branches around the world, including sub-Saharan Africa. It awards scholarships to nationals from African, Asian and European countries, as well as from the New World, to pursue Arabic and Islamic studies in Libyan universities and at the Faculty for the Islamic Appeal. The Association for the Islamic Appeal also organizes conferences, provides financial assistance for the construction of mosques and Islamic training centres, as well as medical help for the destitute, while sending out hundreds of African and Asian preachers to proselytize in Libya and other African countries (Mattes 1993: *passim*).

Libya has often supported local opponents to destabilize African governments. The hegemonic aims of Colonel Ghadaffi have created diplomatic incidents and led to the breaking of diplomatic relationships between Libya and other African countries. In Senegal, Ahmad Khalifa Niass is considered to be one of Ghadaffi's men. Also known as the Ayatollah of Kaolack, he announced at a press conference in October 1979 at the George V Hotel in Paris, the creation of a party whose ambition was to establish an Islamic state (Coulon 1983:139, Magassouba 1985:136). In May 1982, he was arrested and imprisoned for having burnt the French flag during the official visit of President François Mitterand, but was freed shortly afterwards. However, it was a rare incident in Senegal, a country of secular culture and where radical Islam has not been able to take root.

Saudi Arabia has also made a major contribution to the promotion of Arabic language in black Africa. It is difficult to evaluate the Saudi effort because it is transmitted through official channels as well as non-governmental organizations and individual benefactors. According to Fouad al-Farsy (1990:295) Saudi assistance to Third World countries represented 6 per cent of its total GDP. In Africa, 96 percent of this assistance went to Muslim countries until the early 1980s (Nyang 1982:13). There are many organizations that handle this aid to African countries, including the World Muslim League, the Dar al-Ifta, the World Assembly of Muslim Youth (WAMY), the International Federation of Arab and Islamic Schools. Through these organizations, funding is given to Muslim associations, schools and leaders in Africa, Asia and America. At the beginning of the 1980s, there were 2,000 African students attending Saudi universities (Nyang 1982:13), all of them taught in Arabic.

In Tunisia, the sub-Saharan Arabists have usually attended one of two institutions (Bahri 1993:76): the Rakada Lycée or the Theology Faculty of the University of Zeytouna. Like Libya, Tunisia only admitted a few hundred students from black Africa, most of them Senegalese, and this was mainly between 1960 and the mid-1970s. However, some of them were able, during their training, to become familiar with the writings of Islamist thinkers such as the Sudanese Hasan Al-Turabi, the Egyptians Hasan Al-Banna (killed in 1949) and Sayyid Qutb (hanged in 1966), the Pakistanis Abu ʿAla al-Mawdudi (d. 1979) and Rashid Ghannouchi (Bahri 1993:90). Most of the university teaching staff of the Rakada Lycée are Islamists and the sub-Saharan students find brotherly attitudes among them, which they do not find in Tunisian society as a whole. Thus, a certain number of African students have been converted to Islamism during their stay in Tunisia (Bahri 1993:90).

Sudan is another popular destination for African Arabists. Like Mauritania, this country which is half-way between Arabized North Africa and sub-Saharan Africa, is an exception as far as the Arabization of black Africa is concerned. The northern population of Sudan speaks Arabic and is largely Islamized, while the southern populations are predominantly Christian or followers of traditional African religions, and are non-Arabophone. Before it became independent, Sudan received a limited number of Arabists from the British colonies of sub-Saharan Africa. One of the most illustrious was the Nigerian Abubacar Mahmud Gumi (1922-1992), the former grand *qadi* (supreme judge) of Northern Nigeria during the first Republic (1960-1966) and certainly one of the towering figures of the Islamic revival in black Africa in the twentieth century. After the independence of Sudan, there was a policy to promote Islam and the Arabic language in black Africa, which had to be adapted to the limited means of the country. The Sudanese trained young students from these countries, offering them 'a model of modernity that was different from that of the West and that combated the negative imagination of the Arabs and of Islam' (Grandin 1993:98) which had been built up in black Africa by the colonial library. Unlike countries like Saudi Arabia, Egypt, Morocco and Libya, the efforts of Sudan to promote Arabic in black Africa did not seem to be motivated by expansionist aims of seeking the leadership of the Muslim world. According to Grandin (1993:98-99), there were three main reasons that explained Sudanese cultural policy in sub-Saharan Africa: the Sudanese view regarding the low level of training, both in religious fields and in the general education of the African youth; an old tradition of Arab-Islamic proselytization towards neighbouring black populations; and finally, the strong anti-Western and anti-colonial attitudes among the nationalist political elite, constituted in large part of advocates of the Arabization and Islamization of Sudan.

From a Sudanese perspective, religious knowledge is not enough to train preachers capable of playing a decisive role in the Islamization and development of their country of origin (Grandin 1993:99). Importance is given to expertise in scientific and technical fields. So, the elaboration of the curriculum of the African Islamic Centre (*al-markaz al-islami al-ifriqi*) for training Africans took this into account (Grandin 1993:114). There is therefore a clear difference with Al-Azhar, for example, which receives thousands of students from black Africa, but who are mostly oriented towards religious studies.

Created by decree in 1966, the African Islamic Centre was opened in Omdurman in 1967 as an institute affiliated with the Ministry of National Education. It functioned until 1969 when it was closed for eight years (Grandin 1993:107). In 1977, the centre was reopened as in institute that was essentially aimed at religious proselytization (Grandin 1993:113). This development should be seen in the context of the 1970s and the expansion of Islamism in the Muslim world (Kepel 2000 *passim*). Especially in Sudan under the leadership of Hasan Al-Turabi, the Muslim Brotherhood was very popular and recruited many sympathizers from all social backgrounds.

The centre was then attached to the Ministry for Religious Affairs and it recruited from countries in black Africa and Muslim communities outside Africa. Bearing in mind the employment problems experienced by the first generation of African Arabists, the renewed Centre, now based on the outskirts of Khartoum, was careful to train students who were fluent in English or French as well as Arabic (Grandin 1993:108). It also offered basic training in scientific disciplines that enabled graduates to enter a profession or further their training elsewhere after graduation. On returning to their countries, they then had every chance of obtaining professional employment, a pre-condition for credibility. As in the Gulf countries, the centre has also adopted the strategy of recruiting young people from influential families (Grandin 1993:111) and inculcating in them an Islamic ideology that would prepare them for contributing to the reform of their own societies in the sense of greater Islamization.

It should be mentioned that when it reopened, the African Islamic Centre, after considering the different methods of propaganda (communist, missionary and others), saw the need for new methods of proselytization and training missionaries to deal with current challenges. This echoes the more global concern of the Islamic movements and thinkers about the most efficient methods of proselytization. Like the Christian missions, the Islamists concluded that, as well as religious training, it was indispensable to include fields like health care, the creation of clinics and schools and the granting of financial assistance.

Mention should also be made, to conclude this round-up of the networks, issues and contexts in the training of Arabist students, of the fact that attendance at the Arab universities can create two very different attitudes among students when they return to their own country. Some, after witnessing a lesser degree of religiosity in the Arab countries and having suffered from all kinds of racist prejudices (Bahri 1993:89), not only returned as Arabophobes, but they also abandoned practising the Muslim religion. Others, who acquired an in-depth knowledge of Arabic and the Muslim religion and who were fascinated by Islamism, preached a reform in the practice of Islam, if not an Islamic state.

This was all the more the case as the period of the expansion of Islamism corresponded with the considerable increase in the number of African Arabists attending institutions of higher learning in the Arab World.

Nevertheless, the return to the homeland was a disappointment for most of the graduates from Arab countries. Not proficient in Western languages, the first graduates of the 1970s had difficulty in securing jobs. As from the 1980s, some of them began to master Western languages and had a better chance of employment, but they were confronted with the unemployment crisis which spared no graduate of any system. The state, which had been the main supplier of jobs, froze recruitment in public service. While some Arabists managed to become economic or cultural private entrepreneurs, most of them had difficulties in finding satisfactory jobs, as reflected by the poet Cheikh Tidiane Gaye in a work entitled 'Arabist':

Zalamuna wa rabbina zalamuna	They have oppressed us, O God, they have oppressed us
Absat al-haqq fi'l-dunya baramuna	Of the most elementary right they have deprived us

Moreover, although most of them possessed a scholarly certified religious capital, these Arabists were unable to compete for control over religious and social matters with a local religious establishment that had a solid economic base, social capital and access to the state. Partly because they could not secure employment or acquire social influence, they challenged the status quo by advocating greater Arabization and the Islamization of the state – a new political dispensation that would entail greater social recognition for them. This was the African context at the beginning of the 1980s when Islamist movements became visible throughout the Muslim world.

10

Arabists and Islamism

After the colonial conquest, colonial administrations transformed the juridical system in Muslim countries with a view to modernizing it. Much of Islamic penal law, and harsh bodily punishments in particular (such as the amputation of thieves' hands, the stoning of adulterers), were abolished everywhere in Africa. However, the law concerning so-called personal status (*al-akhwal al-shakhsiyya*), which governed marriage, succession, child custody and so on was maintained. The post-colonial African state also adopted secularism as a principle of government.

After decolonization, Third World leaders were inspired by various ideologies in the quest for modernization. For many, it was to be a version of socialism, sometimes liberalism or nationalism. Sub-Saharan Africa, where the great majority of countries are secular, was no exception to the rule. However, independence did not improve the living conditions of African populations. Two decades after the independence of most African countries, not only were the promises for a better future not fulfilled, it was also evident that these countries were undergoing economic decline and social malaise. There were vigorous debates about the origins of the crisis and possible solutions. First, the causes of the decline were identified in the economic policies adopted at independence. Generally speaking, it was assumed that agriculture could not be the engine for development and industrialization should be pursued.

Thus, inspired by development economists, African leaders adopted import-substitution models of industrialisation, with all their panoply of protectionist measures, fixed rates of exchange and appreciation of the value of their currency, rationing foreign exchange through a system of allocation controlled by the state, priority to certain sectors in the allocation of domestic credit, industrialization led by state-owned enterprises, and heavy taxation of agriculture through state-controlled-marketing boards (Lofchie 1994:147-154). Agriculture was so heavily taxed that policies became counter-productive. Industry, which greatly depended on transfers from agriculture, was not long in following suit (Lofchie 1994:147-154).

Incapable of servicing their debt, African countries were forced to accept the humiliating terms of the international financing agencies, the IMF and the World Bank especially, and to implement structural adjustment programmes to obtain the rescheduling of their debts. These programmes meant the dismantling of import substitution industrialization in favour of economic liberalization. At the end of the 1980s, the limited success of the structural adjustment programmes somewhat modified the terms of the debate. Then the donor countries and the Bretton Woods institutions became convinced that the origin of the economic malaise of Africa was political. Consequently, it was necessary to establish systems of 'good governance': to impose accountability of the government to the people, guarantee freedom of expression and of the press, as well as political pluralism. Thus, almost all sub-Saharan countries were obliged to undergo some form of political and economic liberalization.

At the same time as such debates initiated by the donor agencies were going on, there were other ways, far less rational, of assessing the crisis confronting these countries. For example, certain Muslim militant intellectuals (Kepel and Richard 1990) argued that the secularism adopted by Muslim countries in Africa was at the root of the crisis, and was therefore a divine punishment. Consequently, as the Koran stated (11-13), 'God does not change what is in a people before the people change what is in themselves'. What was rather required was a struggle to set up an Islamic state to replace the secular state of Western inspiration. This debate was not confined to a few *ulemas* trained in strictly Islamic universities: individuals from all social categories, including Europhone intellectuals and even one-time Marxists and modernists, accepted this diagnosis. They also accepted the notion that the establishment of an Islamic state was the panacea. The overturning of the Pahlavi monarchy in Iran in 1979, and the creation of an Islamic state in that country, strengthened the conviction of the Islamist intellectuals that their diagnosis was correct.

The first revolution in the Third World that was not subservient to either of the two blocs that dominated the post-World War II period, the upheaval in Iran, had raised hope among many Muslims that Islam could constitute an alternative. In sub-Saharan Africa, at the beginning of the 1980s, belief was rife among the Arabists and, to a lesser extent, the Europhone intellectuals, that the secular state should be dismantled and replaced by political systems based on values prioritizing Islam. Books and journals in Arabic, European and African languages questioned the idea of the secular state and were widely discussed, especially on university campuses. However, at the beginning of the 1990s, the fascination for the Iranian model had much diminished in Africa (Kane and Triaud 1998).

11

Conclusion

Mudimbe's interpretation of what he calls the African gnosis, 'the ideological and scientific discourse on Africa', is based essentially on a Western epistemological order. This is also true of Appiah's analysis of African intellectuals. However, while there is little doubt that there is a Western epistemological order in Africa, it is certainly not as dominant as Mudimbe and Appiah would suggest. Like the great majority of Europhone intellectuals in sub-Saharan Africa, these two authors do not seem aware of their region's important Islamic library. As a result, they do not sufficiently integrate the epistemological references of this Islamic library in their syntheses on the production of knowledge in Africa – which are indeed remarkable. In his book which refers to several hundreds of European and Europhone African authors, Mudimbe (1988:181) mentions only in one paragraph that Islamic sources have always been important in the research for and invention of African paradigms, and that Islamic culture has made a great contribution to the passion for Otherness, particularly in West Africa. In illustrating the importance of these sources, Mudimbe cites six authors: Ibn Hawqal (10th century), Al-Bakri (11th century), Idrisi (12th century), and Ibn Batuta, Ibn Khaldun and Maqrizi (14th century) – all Arab authors. He does not cite any Arabist Africans, some of whose works have been translated into Western languages. Such summary treatment does not do justice to the Islamic library of sub-Saharan Africa consisting of writings in Arabic and in *a'jami*. Medieval Arabic texts about Africa and fundamental books on Islamic knowledge taught in medieval Arabic colleges constitute the nucleus of the Islamic library (see Annexure). This library was enriched by the writings of African scholars in Arabic or *a'jami* of the last five centuries, of those of Arabists trained in African and Arabic countries more recently, and finally the writings of intellectuals fluent in both Arabic and some Western languages.

It is impossible to reconstitute this library completely. As the texts date over centuries and are mostly in the form of circulating manuscripts, only some of them have been transmitted to us while others have perished because of poor conservation conditions. Work on collecting them continues and the documents that have already been gathered attest to an intense intellectual life and important debates on society that are completely ignored by the overwhelming majority of Europhone intellectuals.

Traditional Muslim scholars have left us a library that contains writings in various fields of Islamic sciences, as well as historical documents of all kinds. That the historical documents are invaluable sources for the study of the economic and social history of sub-Saharan Africa is obvious.

Some might argue that the texts concerning traditional Islamic sciences are of little interest for social sciences and humanities scholars, as they are part of a scholastic tradition in which the thinking of the authors is not autonomous. To this objection, there are two counterarguments: firstly, the term 'religion' in the modern West has not the same meaning as that of *din* in Arabic, which is believed to be its equivalent (Asad 1993:1 et seq.). Secondly, the mode of legitimation of knowledge is a function of the epistemological universe in which one is situated.

To corroborate the first counter-argument, let us consider the texts of Maliki jurisprudence (*fiqh maliki*) which take up a large part of the corpus studied here. These texts are not religious in the same sense as canon law in the modern West where positive law governs all aspects of social life. In West Africa, for example, Maliki jurisprudence is the basis of legislation concerning personal status. The ways in which one prays, marries, divorces, or organizes inheritance are aspects of life for dozens of millions who are governed by this jurisprudence. Given the role of Islam in structuring the political and social order of peoples and their imagination, the study of Islamic jurisprudence texts does not have the same epistemological and philosophical meaning as a similar study of canon law in the modern West.

The objection regarding the scholastic nature of many of the texts of this Islamic library poses another important epistemological problem: the legitimation of knowledge which varies according to the epistemological order in which one is located. The Western epistemological order, inherited from the Enlightenment, values originality as a way of legitimizing knowledge. The Islamic epistemological order, according to its classical tradition, which shapes the imagination of the traditional scholars in Africa, emphasizes rather the following of precedent as a way of legitimizing knowledge. This is the case to such an extent that, in order to legitimize themselves, the authors of innovations, who certainly exist in this Islamic tradition, must present their innovation within an established tradition. As a consequence, from the heuristic point of view, the fact that some of these texts fall within the scholastic tradition in no way diminishes their interest, if they are placed in their epistemological context of production.

Underlying these two objections is a more fundamental question, that of a universal definition of the intellectual. Looking at the history of modern Europe and the role that the Enlightenment has played in the intellectual construction of the idea of modernity, the idea of the sovereignty of reason is paramount. The thinking of intellectuals to whom most of this paper is dedicated is not autonomous as such: it is to some extent shaped by religious dogmas. Two observations are in order here. First, the interpretation of texts is not always the same and immutable. In certain circumstances, it can change (Foucault 1969:135) and intellectuals in the Islamic tradition have often shown their capacity to innovate. One example concerns slavery, which the Koran never abolished but which is considered by almost all current Islamic thinkers and theologians as null and void. Thus, the thinking inspired by religion is not as rigid and imprisoned by dogma as is often thought.

Second, the notion of the autonomy of reason is not neutral. It is a philosophical and political position aimed at contesting the dominant beliefs and values of a society at a given historical moment. The intellectual and political agenda of the Enlightenment philosophers was motivated by their desire to contest the traditional figures of authority in pre-modern Europe, particularly the clergy and, to a lesser degree, the monarchy. The educated militants of pre-colonial Islam who denounced the African kings, accusing them of pagan practices or of being bad Muslims, had similar aims, even if they used a different language. In the same way, the Islamists of the post-colonial period blamed the authorities of the modern state (the post-colonial political elites) and the project of a secular society that these elites tried to promote.

The growth of education in Western languages has not led to a decline in Arabic – quite the contrary. In West Africa, the intellectual tradition expressed in Arabic has been greatly reinvigorated through both the modernization of local Arabic teaching and the availability of networks for training Arabists in the Arab countries. While the first generation of Arabists trained in Arabic universities obtained mainly religious knowledge, more recent Arabists, as in Sudan, enjoy many more opportunities, including the possibility to learn Western languages and study the hard sciences. Some of the Arabists, conscious of the importance of European languages, are doing their best to acquire a mastery of them. More open-minded than most of the pure products of the traditional Arab-Islamic scholarship, some (although not all) of the new Arabists are computer literate and are aware of cutting edge developments in the new information and communication technology. They are creating journals, newspapers and magazines. In Senegal, the founder and president of one of the most important press groups, Sidi Lamine Niasse, is an Arabist by training. At first, the daily product of his press group, *Walfadjri,* was an Islamic information bulletin imprisoned in the waffle of Islamist militants. In time, the bulletin became a daily in French and, with its team of highly professional journalists, one of the most respected papers in Senegal. The group's radio, Walf FM, is also one with the largest audiences in Senegal, transmitting programmes not only in French but also in local Senegalese languages. The press group has recently acquired a television station. Sidi Lamine Niasse has written books and numerous articles in French.

To return to the debate started up in the introduction, while it is true that the expanded colonial library structures a Western epistemological order that shapes the thinking of Europhone intellectuals, it is no less true that the expanded Islamic library is creating an Islamic space of meaning. This library contains the writings of non-Europhone and 'hybrid' intellectuals. Among the latter is a group that studied Arabic first and then Western languages, and another group who did it the other way round, plus a third group that studied Arabic and Western languages at one and the same time. Some intellectuals are at home in several intellectual traditions: for example, the late Amadou Hampathé Bâ and Saada Umar Touré in Mali, Amar Samb, El-Hadji Madior Cissé in Senegal, Abubacar Gumi, Haliru Binji and Naibi Suleyman Wali in Nigeria. These personalities are unquestionably well-known intellectuals who are neither just Europhone nor just Arabophone. They are polyglots, able to express themselves in several scholarly languages. And whether they are Europhones, non-Europhones or 'hybrids', these intellectuals share an Islamic space of meaning.

Appendix I

A Research Project

The intellectual history of sub-Saharan Africa cannot be reduced to a study of Europhone intellectuals alone. It is important to study the other intellectual traditions, and therefore necessary to continue the listing of texts in non-Western languages, including Arabic and *a'jami*. This task is all the more urgent in that some of these writings have not been microfilmed or published. They are rotting away in private libraries in poor conditions and risk being lost forever.

It is important to overcome two kinds of barriers in the effort to de-compartmentalize knowledge and renew our thinking about the production of knowledge in Africa. The first barrier is disciplinary: there is no conversation between intellectual historians of sub-Saharan Islam such as Islamicists and Europhone social scientists concerned with the sociology of knowledge, such as Mudimbe or Appiah. From reading the works of both, it is obvious that they hardly communicate at all. As discussed earlier, there exists abundant information about the Islamic library in Western languages. But the rare Europhone intellectuals who mention Arabic sources in the history of Africa cite hardly more than the two *tawarikh* of Mahmoud Kaᶜti and Abderhamane Al-Saᶜdi (*Tarikh al-Fattash* and *Tarikh al-Sudan*).

The other kind of barrier is linguistic, and it separates the Europhone from the non-Europhone intellectual. To overcome it, there has to be an effort to collect and translate Arabic and *a'jami* texts into Western languages, particularly those dating from the pre-colonial or colonial periods, of which there are very few copies extant. Very praiseworthy initiatives are underway in Africa, which complement the work carried out in Western countries. Among them, two – both focussing on Mali – are worthy of mention.

In August 2002, the Malian Association for Research and Action for Development organized an international symposium on the theme *Les chemins de l'encre* (Ink Paths). It aimed at 'setting up and running an institutional arrangement for the protection, exchange and conservation of the corpus of ancient African manuscripts', and at starting 'the sharing of experience in conservation and the initiatives in scientific research to safeguard and promote the written heritage'.[10] The other initiative was taken after the visit to Mali of the South African President Thabo Mbeki in November 2001, following which he pledged to support the preservation of Malian manuscripts. South Africa and Mali have ratified an agreement called the Timbuktu Bi-National Presidential Project: South Africa and Mali. It aims at restoring all the libraries and collections of manuscripts in Timbuktu, and is already at work.[11] The cost is estimated at R320,000,000.

The number of books, newspapers, journals, magazines and other publications in Arabic and African languages, in *ajami* and in Latin characters, has grown enormously over the last two decades. The study on non-Europhone intellectuals must therfore pay particular attention to the growth of this literature, its dissemination networks, its authors and its contents. Unlike the manuscripts upon which numerous researchers are working, there has been no systematic attempt, so far, to collect this more recent printed material.

There should also be a study of the positions taken by non-Europhone intellectuals on some universal principles invoked by Enlightenment thinkers to see how the former approach the notion of 'modernity', and whether this approach has changed over time. Most contemporary Islamic movements have appropriated modern technology. Is their acceptance of modernity limited to the use of technology alone or does it include the recognition of the universality of certain values and freedoms and a greater autonomy for reason? The answer to this question cannot be very clear-cut as the Islamist movements are far from being monolithic. Because classical Islamic thought recognizes the need for innovation, the principle that legitimizes it is *ijtihad* (intellectual effort exerted to find solutions to new problems and challenges that are faced by the Muslim community).

Contemporary struggles within Islamist movements oppose conservatives to the partisans of a greater opening up. Alongside Islamists educated in the traditional system, there are also others who are products of the modern world; either through a modern education or through the combination of traditional and modern training. Some have been followers of secular ideologies (socialism, communism, liberalism) before converting to Islamism. The outlook of the latter on the modern world can continue to evolve, but even among the purest products of the traditional system of education, there are audacious thinkers capable of rethinking the 'dogmas'. It is thus imperative to move beyond the notion that Arabists, even if they have been completely trained in the classical tradition, are prisoners of dogma from which they cannot free themselves.

Similarly, one might wonder whether the decline of radical Islamism, which can be seen almost everywhere in the Muslim world, signifies the triumph of the more open-minded groups among the militant Muslims. This question can be studied by analyzing the ongoing conversations among militants. Radio programmes, newspapers, books and journals in the languages of communication of these intellectuals would be appropriate material for such an analysis.

As we are dealing with the Islamic intellectual tradition, its recent impact on African society would merit study. To do this, one should go beyond analyzing the manuscripts and printed works to study the way in which groups re-appropriate, manipulate, transform and adapt Islamic concepts to promote their agenda. Over the last decades, the proposal for the inclusion of *sharīʿa* in the Nigerian Federal Constitution has provoked one of the most stormy debates in post-colonial Nigeria, started with the application of 'full shariʿa' in Zamfara state. Since then, most other states of northern Nigeria, under the pressure of public opinion, have adopted the same approach. Thus, the questions that arise from the so-called 'religious' texts are part of the major debates on society in post-colonial Africa. They need careful study.

The development of new information and communication technologies facilitates a more rapid dissemination of debates on Islamic knowledge. The different transmission systems should be identified and studied systematically. Radio-cassettes, video-cassettes, radio and television programmes have integrated non-Western languages into an oral and visual basis, and the debates taking place on the worldwide web have become commonplace.

A study of non-European intellectuals and their knowledge in sub-Saharan Africa should not be limited to the Arabic intellectual tradition and to the *dʾjami*. It is also necessary to include those writing in African languages transcribed in Latin characters. Apart from West Africa, with which this study has been mainly concerned, it would be advisable to integrate the views of specialists from East Africa, the islands of the Indian Ocean and Southern and Central Africa, if not North Africa, where there is, though to a lesser degree, a marginalization of non-Europhone intellectuals.

The work of such a group should not be restricted to those who write. It should also include other actors who are making the world intelligible (Copans 1993:17), including those who do not necessarily belong to the Europhone or Arab-Islamic intellectual traditions.

Such a research group should examine the extent to which intellectuals belonging to the different linguistic traditions share the same epistemological points of reference. Intellectuals who are trained today in the social and human sciences in Arabic countries or the Arab Universities of Niger and Uganda share the same space of meaning as those trained at Berkeley or the Sorbonne, even if they do not speak English or French. The Arabists training in sociology in the Arab universities know as much about Weber, Marx and Durkheim (who have been translated into Arabic) as the sociology students of Nanterre or the University of Dakar.

Moreover, there are graduates who have received all their training in the traditional Islamic schools who are not however restricted to medieval theology. They have been listening to foreign radio programmes in Arabic or African languages for decades now and they are thoroughly conversant with the most recent debates on modernity and globalization. They have therefore the same degree of sophistication as the intellectuals trained in other traditions. Thus, even if the corpus of the traditional Islamic teaching remains unchanged (see Annexure), it would be a mistake to say that those who have received such training in 1900, 1950 and 2000 have exactly the same epistemological points of reference.

In the same way, because of the diffusion of information programmes in African languages (the BBC, for example, has been broadcasting in Hausa since the 1950s), it is not rare to find individuals in Northern Nigeria without any formal intellectual training able to undertake a completely coherent discourse on globalization, structural adjustment, political liberalization and secularism in Hausa. What is true in Nigeria also goes for the other African countries where radio, television and newspapers are making considerable efforts to spread maximum information and other programmes in non-Western languages. The growth of the new information and communication technologies and the growing place of national languages in this framework give the impression that among the speakers of non-Western languages, there are numerous people who share the same space of meaning as Europhone intellectuals.

Finally, it should be said that the English, French and Portuguese languages have evolved in Africa to express local ideas and concerns. For example, some phrases in the French or English spoken in Africa may not be understood in France or in England. Thus, the very notion of Europhone intellectuals is problematic and should be reconsidered.

Given the breadth of this research agenda and the pluri-disciplinary approach required to pursue it, no single research methodology can be proposed. Some researchers will rely more on quantitative methods, other on qualitative ones and a third category will combine the two. Some members of the research group will be Europhone intellectuals and others non-Europhone, and still others will be a blend of the two. Such collaboration, one hopes, will help change the terms of the debate on the production of knowledge among both Europhone and non-Europhone intellectuals.

Appendix II

Some Elements of the Corpus of Traditional Arab-Islamic Teaching

Koranic Exegesis

- *Tafsir al-jalalayn* of Jalal al-din Al-Suyuti (died in 1505) and of Jalal al-din Mahalli
- *Hashiyat al-Sawi*, which is a commentary on *Tafsir al-jalalayn*)

Hadith

- *Jami al-sahih* of Muhammad b. Isma'il Bukhari (died in 870), a work known as the *Sahih* of Bukhari
- *Jami al-sahih* of Abu 'l-Husayn b. Hajjaj al-Qushayri al-Nisaburi (died in 875), a work known as the Muslim *Sahih*

Sufism

- *Jawahir al ma'ani wa bulugh al-amani fi fayd Ahmad al-Tijani* of Ali Harzim Barrada (died in 1799)
- *Rimah hizb al-rahim* of Umar al-Futi (died in 1864)
- *Al-Qasq'id al-'ashriyat fi 'l-nasa'ih al-diniyya wa 'l-hikam al-zuhdiyya* of 'Abd al-Rahman b. Yakhlaftan al-Fazazi known as Al-Fazazi (died in 1230)

Grammar

- *Al-muqaddima al-ajurrumiyya* by 'Abdallah b. Muhammad al-Sanhaji known as Ibn Ajurrum (died in 1323)
- *Alifyya fi 'l-nahw* of Jamal-al-din Muhammad b. 'Abd Allah al-Tai al-Jayyani, known as Ibn Malik (died in 1273)

- *Muqadimma al-ʿashmawiyya* of ʿAbd al-Bari al-Rifaʿi al-ʿAshmawi (16ᵗʰ century)

- *Lamiyyat al-afʿal* of Jamal-al-din Muhammad b. ʿAbd Allah al-Tai al-Jayyani, known as Ibn Malik (died in 1273)

- *Irshad al-salik* of ʿAbd al-Rahman b. Muhammad Ibn ʿAskar al-Baghdadi (died in 1332)

Panegyrics of the Prophet

- *Al-Kawakib al-duriyya bi fi madh khayr al-bariyya*, also known as the *al-burda* of Sharaf al-din Muhammad al-Busiri al-Sanhaji (died in 1296)

- *Dala'il al-khayrat wa shawariq al-anwar fi dhikr al-salat ʿala al-nabi al-mukhtar* of Muhammad b. Suleyman al-Jazuli (died in 1465)

- *Al-Qasa'id al-ʿishriniyya fi madh sayyidina Muhammad* of ʿAbd al-Rahman b. Yakhlaftan al-Fazazi known as Al-Fazazi (died in 1230)

Maliki Jurisprudence

- *Mukhtasar fi 'l furuʿ* of Diya al-Din Khalil b. Ishaq al-Jundi (died in 1374)

- *Risala* of ʿAbd Allah b. Abi Zayd ʿAbd al-Rahman al-Qayrawani (died in 996)

- *Mukhtasar fi-'l-ibadat ʿala madhhab al-imam Malik* of ʿAbd al-Rahman b. Muhammad al-Saghir al-Akhdari (died in 1585)

Theology

- *Al-muqaddima al-jazariyya fi ʿilm al-tawhid* of Shams al-Din 'Khayr al-Dimashqi al-Jazari, known as Ibn al-Jazari (died in 1429)

- *Al-jumal* (also called *al-murshid* or Wusta) of Muhammad b. Yusuf al-Hasani al-Sanusi al-Tilimsani (died in 1486)

- *Umm al-barahin* (Source of proofs), also known as *al-sughra* (little dogma) of Muhammad b. Yusuf al-Hasani al-Sanusi al-Tilimsani (died in 1486)

- *ʿAqida ahl al-tawhid wa 'l-tasdid, al-mukhrija min zulumat al-jahl wa raqabat al-taqlid* known also under the name *al-kubra* (great dogma) of Muhammad b. Yusuf al-Hasani al-Sanusi al-Tilimsani (died in 1486)

- *Ilya ʿulum al-din* of Abu Hamid Muhammad b. Muhammad Al-Ghazali (died in 1111)

- *Al-madkhal ila tanmiyat al-aʿmal bi bahsin al-niyyat* of Muhammad b. Muhammad al-Hajj al-Fasi al-Adbari (died in 1336)

- *Urjuzat al-wildam* of Hahya b. ʿUmar al-Qurtubi (died in 1171)

- *Al-Tuhfa al-wardiyya* of ʿUmar b. Muzaffar al-Shafiʿi, also called Ibn al-Wardi (died in 1349).

Notes

1. In the meaning given it by Foucault (1969-70), the library refers to 'a documentary field that comprises books and treatises traditionally recognized as 'valid' in a specific field. The library also contains a mass of statistical information, as well as a collection of accounts and observations published or transmitted, that concern this field. As they constitute a group of statements 'belonging to the same discursive formation (Foucault 1969:44 et seq.), the writings of a given library create a system of representation'.
2. In the Western meaning of the term, the birth of the social sciences can be traced to the works of Western philosophers such as Montesquieu, Diderot, Rousseau, Adam Smith, David Hume, just to cite some of them, whose common denominator is their critical attitude towards the structures of the authorities of medieval Western Europe, i.e. the monarchy and the clergy. At the end of the nineteenth century, the contributions of authors like Emile Durkheim, Max Weber, and Ferdinand Tonnies gave to the social sciences their current form, i.e. a focus on the study of the real world as opposed to the speculation characteristic of the Enlightenment philosophers, and the emergence of different specializations created by the intellectual division of labour. See Stuart Hall, David Held, Don Hubert, Kenneth Thompson, *Modernity. An Introduction to Modern Societies*, Cambridge, Mass., Blackwell, 1996:4.
3. Commenting on the article of Achille Mbembe 'African Modes of Self-Writings' in *Identity, Culture and Politics: An Afro-Asian Dialogue*, No. 2, 2001:1-35, Nira Wickramansinghe (2000:38) points out that the title 'African modes' is problematic: it would make no sense in Asia because there no-one would identify themselves as Asian.
4. There were 300 bishoprics in North Africa before the invasion of the Vandals who de-Christianized the region, thus preparing the terrain for the expansion of Islam.
5. See the later section on Political/Intellectual Revolutions.
6. Accessed on October 2002.
7. Even if it is better known as the *Burda* (Mantle, in Arabic), the title of this panegyric of the Prophet is *al-kawakib al-duriyya fi madh khayr al-bariyya* (The shining planets, or the eulogy to the best of all creatures). Its author was Sharaf al-din al-Busiri al-Sanhaji (1226-1294). For a French translation, see Boubakeur (1980).
8. The name of the movement *Jam'at izalat al-bida wa iqamat al-sunna* (The Society for the Removal of Heresy and Reinstatement of Tradition), which is the largest single reform movement in post-colonial West Africa, is inspired by the title of this book (Kane 2003).
9. Our information on this university is based on data supplied by this author.
10. See the papers of the international symposium.
11. See 'Timbuktu Bi-national Presidential Project: South Africa and Mali', in *Jamiatul Ulama Transvaal Noticeboard*, 22 February 2002 in www.islamsa.org.za/noticeboard/html.

Bibliography

Abdullahi, Shehu Umar, 1984, *On the Search for a Viable Political Culture*, Kaduna, NNN Commercial Printing Department.

Abitbol, Michel, 1982, *Tombouctou au milieu du XVIIIe siècle d'après la chronique de Mawlay al-Qasim b. Mawlay Sulayman* (translation Michel Abitbol), Paris, Maisonneuve et Larose.

Abu Bakr, Ali, 1972, *Al-thaqafa al-carabiyya fi Nijeriya*, Beyrouth, Mu'assassat ʿAbd al-Hafid al-Bassat.

Adamu, Mahdi and Kirk-Greene, A., M. M., (eds.), 1986, *Pastoralists of the West African Savanna*, Manchester, Manchester University Press in association with the International African Institute.

Ahmed, Hussein, 1992, "The Historiography of Islam in Ethiopia" *Journal of Islamic Studies*, vol. 3, 1, janvier, 15-46.

Ahmed, Hussein, 1998a, "Islamic Literature and Religious Revival in Ethiopia", *Islam et sociétés au sud du Sahara*, 12, 89-108.

Ahmed, Hussein, 1998b, "Islamic Literature in Ethiopia: A Short Overview", *Ethiopian Journal of Languages and Literature*, 8, 25-37.

Al Farsy, Fouad, 1990, *Modernity and Tradition: The Saudi Equation*, London and New York, Kegan Paul International.

Al-Burtuli, 1989, *Fath al-Shakur fi macrifat dyan ulama al-Tarkrur*, Beyrouth, Dar al-gharb al-islami.

Al-Busiri, Sharafu-d-Dîn, 1980, *Al-Burda* (le manteau), (Hamza Boubakeur transl.), Montpellier, Imprimerie TIP.

Al-Hajj, M. A., 1968, "A Seventeenth Century Chronicle on the Origins and Missionary Activities of the Wangarawa", *Kano Studies*, (1), 4, 7-16.

Al-Hajj, M. A., 1973, "The Mahdist Tradition in Northern Nigeria", PhD. thesis in history, Ahmadu Bello University.

Al-Shinqiti, Ahmad al-Amin, 1989, *Al-Wasit fi tarajim udaba al-Shinqit*, Cairo and Nouakchott, Maktabat al-khanji & Mu'assasa al-Munir.

Al-Zirikli, Khayr al-din, 1990, *Al-Aʿlam. Qamus tarajim li-ashhur al-rijal wa 'l-nisa min al-ʿarab wa 'l-mustaʿribin wa 'l-mustashriqin*, Beyrouth, Dar al-ʿilm li 'l-malayin.

Anderson, Benedict, 1991, *Imagined Communities: Reflection on the Origin and Spread of Nationalism*, New York, Verso, 3rd edition.

Andrjewski, B., Pilaszewicz S. And Tyloch, W, 1985, *Literature in African Languages*, Warsaw, Cambridge.

Anyang' Nyong'o, P., 1987, "Some critical notes on Problems in Third World Countries of the Working Relationship Between Intellectuals and the State", paper delivered at the international conference "Intellectuals, the State and Imperialism", Harare, University of Zimbabwe, 20-22 October.

Asad, Talal, 1993, *Genealogies of Religion: Discipline and Reasons of Power in Christianity and Islam*, Baltimore and London, The Johns Hopkins University Press.

Asani, Ali S., 1995, "Urdu Literature", in Esposito L. (ed.), *The Oxford Encyclopeadia of the Modern Islamic World*, New York, Oxford University Press, vol. 4, pp. 289-296.

Aschcroft, Bill, Griffiths, Gareth and Tiffin Helen (dirs), 1995, *The Post-colonial Studies Reader,* London, Routledge.

Bahri, Jalal, 1993, "Le lycée de Rekada: Une filière de formation pour les arabisants d'Afrique noire en Tunisie", in Otayek René (*dir*), *Le radicalisme islamique au sud du Sahara. Dá wa, arabisation et critique de l'Occident*, Paris, Karthala, 75-95.

Barkindo, Bawuro, 1985, "Early States of the Central Sudan: Kanem, Borno and Some of their Neighbours to c. 1500 AD", in Ade Ajayi J. F. and Crowder Michael, *History of West Africa*, London, Longman, 3e édition, pp. 225-254.

Bathily, Abdoulaye, 1994, "The West African State in Historical Perspective", in Osaghae Eghosa (ed.) *Between State and Civil Society in Africa*, Dakar, CODESRIA, 41-74.

Bathily, Abdoulaye, 1987, "Intellectuals and the State in West Africa: A Historical Perspective", paper delivered at the international conference "Intellectuals, the State and Imperialism", Harare, University of Zimbabwe, 20-22 October.

Belloncle, Guy, 1984, *La question éducative en Afrique noire*, Paris, Karthala.

Bibliothecaires du Cedrab (comps.), 1998, *Handlist of Manuscripts in the Centre de documentation et de recherches historiques Ahmad Baba Timbuctu*, London, Al-Furqan, vol. 5, mss 6000 to 9000.

Bibliothécaires du Cedrab (comps.) and Al-ᶜAbbas ᶜAbd al-Mushin (ed.), 1998, *Handlist of Manuscripts in the Centre de documentation et de recherches historiques Ahmad Baba Timbuctu*, London, Al-Furqan, vol. 4, mss 4500 to 6000.

Bibliothécaires du Cedrab (comps.) and ᶜAl-Abbas ᶜAbd al-Mushsin (ed.), 1997, *Handlist of Manuscripts in the Centre de documentation et de recherches historiques Ahmad Baba Timbuctu*, London, Al-Furqan, vol. 3, manuscrits numéros 3000 à 4500.

Bibliothécaires du Cedrab (comps.) and Al-ᶜAbbas ᶜAbd al-Mushsin (ed.), 1996, *Handlist of Manuscripts in the Centre de Documentation et de Recherches Historiques Ahmad Baba Timbuctu*, London, Al-Furqan, vol. 2, mss 1500 to 3000.

Bousbina, Said, 1989, "Les mérites de la Tijaniyya d'après "Rimah" d'al Hajj Umar", *Islam et sociétés au sud du Sahara*, 3, pp. 253-259.

Boyd, Jean, Mack Beverly, 1997, *Collected Works of Nana Asma'u, Daughter of Usman dan Fodiyo*, East Lansing, Michigan State University Press.

Boyd, J., 1989, *The Caliph's Sister Nana Asma'u 1793-1865: Teacher, Poet and Islamic Leader*, London, Frank Cass.

Boyd, Jean, 1986 "The Fulani Women Poets", in Adamu Mahdi & Kirk-Greene A. M. M. (eds.) *Pastoralists of the West African Savanna*, Manchester, Manchester University Press in association with the International African Institute.

Brenner, Louis, 1997, "Becoming Muslim in Soudan Français", in Robinson David & Triaud Jean-Louis, *Le Temps des marabouts. Itinéraires et stratégies islamiques en Afrique occidentale v.1880-1960*, Paris, Karthala, pp. 467-492

Brenner, Louis, 1992, "The Jihad Debate between Sokoto and Borno, Historical Analysis of Islamic Political Discourse in Nigeria", in Ade Ajayi J. F. and Peel J. D. Y (eds.), *People and Empires in African History*, London, Longmans, 21-43.

Brenner, Louis, 1985, *Réflexion sur le savoir islamique en Afrique noire*, Bordeaux, Centre d'étude d'Afrique noire.

Brockelman, Carl, 1943-49, Gesc*hichte der Arabischen Literatur*, Leiden, E. J. Brill, 2 volumes, 2nd edition.

Brockelman, Carl, 1937-42, *Geschichte der Arabischen Literatur*, Leiden, E.J. Brill, 3 volumes, Supplemenbanden.

Bruno-Jailly, Joseph,1999, *Djenné d'hier à demain*, Bamako, Editions Donniya.

Bahija, Chadli (ed.), 1996, *Infaq al-maysur fi ta'rikh Bilad al-Takrur of Muhammad Bello*, Rabat, Institut d'études africaines.

Chakrabarty, Dipesh, 1999, "Postcolonialité et artifice de l'histoire: Qui parle au nom du passé indien ?", in Diouf Mamadou (ed.) *L'historiographie indienne en débat: Colonialisme, nationalisme et sociétés postcoloniales*, Paris, Karthala, 73-107, translated by Ousmane Kane.

Collard, Chantal, 1982, "Destin et éducation traditionnelle des enfants guidar", in Santerre, R. & Mercier-Tremblay C. (dirs.), *La Quête du savoir: Essais pour une anthropologie de l'éducation camerounaise*, Montréal, Les Presses de l'université de Montréal, pp. 72-103.

Copans, Jean, 1993, "Intellectuels visibles, intellectuels invisibles", *Politique africaine*, 51, octobre, pp. 7-25.

Coulon, Christian, 1983, *Les musulmans et le pouvoir en Afrique noire*, Paris, Karthala.

Cuoq, Joseph, 1975, *Recueil des sources arabes concernant l'Afrique occidentale du VIIIe au XVIe siecle*, Paris, Editions du centre national de la recherche scientifique, 1985.

Diallo, Thierno, Mbacké Mame Bara, Trifcovic Mirjana, Barry Boubacar, 1966, "Catalogue des manuscrits de l'IFAN: Fonds Vieillard, Gaden, Breviem Figaret, Shaykh Musa Kamara et Cremer en langues arabe, peule et voltaique", Dakar, IFAN (catalogues et documents, 20).

Diouf, Mamadou, 1993 "Les intellectuels face à l'entreprise démocratique: Entre la citoyenneté et l'expertise", *Politique africaine*, 51, octobre, pp. 35-47.

Djebbar, Ahmed, 2001, *Une histoire de la science arabe*, Entretiens avec Jean Rosmorduc, Paris, Seuil.

Eickelman, Dale and Piscatori James, 1996, *Muslim Politics*, Princeton, Princeton University Press.

El-Hamel, 1992, "Fath ash-shakur, hommes de lettres, disciples et enseignement dans le Takrur du début du XVIe au début du XIXe siècles", Ph.D thesis in history, University Paris I.

El-Masri, F. H., 1978, (ed. & transl.), *Bayan wujub al-hijra 'ala 'l-'ibad of 'Uthman b. Fudi*, Khartoum, Khartoum University Press & Oxford University Press.

Encyclopedia of Islam I, 1913-42, Leiden, E. J. Brill.

Encyclopedia of Islam ii, 1960-2004, Leiden, E.J. Brill.

Epelboin, Alain and Hames, Constant, 1993, "Trois vêtements talismaniques provenant du Sénégal (Décharge de Pikine)", *Bulletin d'études orientales*, tome xliv, 217-241.

Fafunwa, A. Babs, 1974, *History of Education in Nigeria*, Ibadan, NPS Educational Publishers Ltd.

Faure, Edgar (ed.), 1972, *Apprendre à être*, Paris, Fayard & Unesco.

Feierman, Steven, 1990, *Peasant Intellectuals. Anthropology and History in Tanzania*, Madison, The University of Wisconsin.

Foucault, Michel, 1969, *L'archéologie du savoir*, Paris, Gallimard.

Furley, O. W. and Watson, T., 1978, *A History of Education in East Africa*, New York, London & Lagos, NOK Publishers.

Furniss, Graham, 1990, *Poetry, Prose and Popular Culture in Hausa*, Washington DC., Smithsonian Institution Press.

Galandanci, Ahmad Said, 1982, *Haraka al-lugha al-'arabiyya wa adabiha fi Nijerya*, Cairo, Dar al-maᶜarif.

Genest, Serge & Santerre, Renaud, 1982, "L'école franco-arabe au Nord-Cameroun", in Santerre, R. & Mercier-Tremblay C. (eds.) *La Quête du savoir: Essais pour une anthropologie de l'éducation camerounaise*, Montréal, Les Presses de l'Université de Montréal, pp. 372-395.

Genest, Serge, 1982, " Savoir traditionnel chez les forgerons mafa", in Santerre, R. & Mercier-Tremblay C. (eds.) *La Quête du savoir: Essais pour une anthropologie de l'éducation camerounaise*, Montréal, Les Presses de l'université de Montréal, 147-179.

Ghali, Nouredine, Mahibou, Sidi Mohammed and Brenner Louis, 1985, *Inventaire de la bibliothèque umarienne de Ségou* (conservée à la bibliothèque nationale), Paris, Editions du CNRS.

Girma, Amare, 1975, "Aims and Purposes of Church Education in Ethiopia", *Education in East Africa*, (5), 1, 43-56.

Good, Charles M., 1987, *Ethncomedical Systems in Africa: Patterns of Traditional Medicine in Rural and Urban Kenya*, London & New York, The Guiliford Press.

Goody, Jacques, 1968, *Literacy in Traditional Societies*, Cambridge, Cambridge University Press.

Grandin, Nicole, 1993, "Al-markaz al-islami al-ifriqi bi 'l-Khartoum: La République du Soudan et la propagation de l'islam en Afrique noire (1977-1991)", in Otayek René (*ed.*), *Le radicalisme islamique au sud du Sahara. Daᶜwa, arabisation et critique de l'Occident*, Paris, Karthala, 75-95.

Gumi, Sheikh Abubacar (with Tsiga A. Ismail), 1993, *Where I stand*, Ibadan, Kaduna, Lagos, Oweri, Spectrum Book Limited.

Hagenbucher-Sacripanti, F., 1992, *Santé et rédemption par les génies du Congo: La médecine traditionnelle selon le mvulusi*, Paris, Publisud.

Haidara, Abdelkader Mamma (comp.) and Fuad Sayyid Ayman (ed.), 2000, *Catalogue of manuscripts in Mamma Haidara Library*, London, Al-Furqan, three volumes.

Haïdara, Ismaël Diadie, 1999, *Les Juifs à Tombouctou: Recueil des sources écrites relatives au commerce juif à Tombouctou au XIXe siècle*, Bamako, Editions Donniya.

Hall, Stuart, 1996, "The West and Rest: Discourse and Power", in Hall Stuart, Held David, Hubert Don and Thompson Kenneth, "Modernity. *An Introduction to Modern Societies*, New York, Blackwell.

Hames, Constant, 1987, "Taktub ou la magie de l'écriture islamique: Textes Soninke à usage magique", *Arabica*, tome xxxiv, 305-325.

Hames, Constant, 1993, "Entre recette magique d'Al-Buni et prière islamique d'Al-Ghazali: Textes talismaniques d'Afrique occidentale", in De Surgy Albert (ed.) *Fétiches II. Puissance des objets, charme des mots*, Paris, Systèmes de pensée en Afrique noire, Cahier 12, 187-233.

Hames, Constant, 1997 (a), "L'art talismanique en Islam d'Afrique occidentale: Personnes, supports, procédés, transmission. Analyse anthropologique et islamologique d'un corpus de talismans à écriture", PhD thesis, Paris, Ecole pratique des hautes études.

Hames, Constant, 1997 (b), "Le Coran talismanique: De l'Arabie des origines à l'Afrique occidentale contemporaine. Délimitation et inventaire des textes et des procédés linguistiques utilisés", in De Surgy Albert, *Religion et pratiques de puissance*, Paris, L'Harmattan, 139-160.

Harrow, Kenneth, 2000, "Islamic Literature in Africa", in Levtzion Nehemia and Pouwels Randall, *The History of Islam in Africa*, Athens, Oxford, Cape Town, Ohio University Press, James Currey, David Philip, 519-544

Hasseb, Khayr El-Din, 1989, *The Arabs of Africa*, London, Sydney, Dover, New Hampshire, Croom Helm & Centre for Arab Unity Studies.

Helen, Bradford, 1983, "Organic Intellectuals or Petty Bourgeois Opportunists: The Social Nature of ICU Leadership in the Countryside", paper presented at the African Studies Institute, University of Witwatersrand, 6 June.

Heymouski, Adam and Ould Hamidoun Moukhtar, 1965-1966, *Catalogue provisoire des manuscrits préservés en Mauritanie*, Nouakchott & Stockholm.

Hiskett, Mervyn and Knappert Jan, 1985, "African Languages and Literature", in Esposito J. (ed.), *The Oxford Encyclopeadia of the Modern Islamic World*, New York, Oxford University Press, vol. 1.

Hiskett, Mervyn, 1975, *A History of Hausa Islamic Verses*, London.

Hiskett, Mervyn, 1977, *An Anthology of Hausa Political Verse*, (Hausa Texts edited and annotated), Evanston, Northwestern University Africana Library AFRI L893.721.

Honey, Rex and Okafor Stanley, 1998, *Hometown Associations: Indigenous Knowledge and development in Nigeria*, London, IT Publications.

Horton, Robin, 1985, "Stateless Societies in the History of West Africa", in Ade Ajayi J. F. and Crowder Michael, *History of West Africa*, London, Longman, vol. 1, 3rd edition, pp. 87-128.

Horton, Robin, 1994, *Patterns of Thought in Africa and the West: Essays on magic, religion and science*, Cambridge, Cambridge University Press.

Hunwick John, 1960-2004, "Timbuctu", *Encyclopedia of Islam II*, Leiden, E.J. Brill.

Hunwick, John, 1992, "An Introduction to the Tijaniyyah Path: Being an Annotated translation of the Chapter Headings of the Kitab al-Rimah of Al-Hajj Umar," *Islam et sociétés au sud du Sahara*, 6, 17-32.

Hunwick, John (comp.), 2002, *Arabic Literature of Africa: The Writings of Western Sudanic Africa,* Leiden, New York, Cologne, E. J. Brill.

Hunwick, John (comp.), 1995, *Arabic Literature of Africa. The Writings of Central Sudanic Africa,* Leiden, New York, Cologne, E. J. Brill.

Hunwick, John (ed. with an introduction and commentary) 1985, *Shar'a in Songhai: The Replies of Al-Maghili to the Questions of Askia al-Hajj Muhammad*, Oxford, Oxford University Press.

Hunwick, John, 1964, "A New Source for the Study of biography of Ahmad Baba al-Timbuctu (1556-1627)", *BSOAS*, vol XXVII, 3, pp. 568-593.

Hunwick, John, 1997, "Towards a History of the Islamic Intellectual Tradition in West Africa down to the Nineteenth Century", *Journal for Islamic Studies*, vol. 17, 4-27.

Hunwick, John, 1999 (a), "The Arabic Manuscript Heritage of the Niger Bend Region," Report of a field trip in Timbuctu.

Hunwick, John, 1999 (b), *Timbuctu & the Songhai Empire: Al-Sa'di's Tarikh al-Sudan down to 1613 & Other Contemporary Documents*, E. J. Brill.

Ihekweazu, E., 1985, *Traditional and Modern Culture*, Enugu, Fourth Dimension Publishing Co. Ltd.

Jega, Attahiru, 1994, *Nigerian Academics under Military Rule*, Stockholm, University of Stockholm, Department of Political Science.

Jinju, M. H., *Hausa Medicinal Plants and Therapy*, Zaria, Gaskiya Corporation Ltd., 1990.

Ka, Thierno and Mbacké, Khadim, 1994, "Nouveau catalogue des manuscrits de l'IFAN",*Islam et sociétés au sud du Sahara*, 8, 165-199.

Ka, Thierno, 1982, "L'enseignement arabe au Sénégal. L'Ecole de Pir-Saniokhor. Son histoire et son rôle dans la culture arabo-islamique au Sénégal du XVIIe au XXe siècle", Université de Paris Sorbonne (Paris IV) Ph.D thesis in history.

ka'ti, Mahmud, 1964, *Tarikh al-Fattash fi akhbar al-buldan wa 'l-juyush wa akabir al-nas* (translation. O. Houdas and M. Delafosse, Paris, 1913; Paris, Maisonneuve et Larose.

Kahhala, Umar Rida, *Mu'jam al-mu'allifin*, Beyrouth, Dar ihya al-turath al-'arabi, 1958, 15 vols.

Kamal, Youssouf, 1987, *Monumenta Carthographica Africae et Aegypty*, Frankfort am Main, Institut Geschischte der Arabish-Islamischen Wissenschaften an der Johann wolfgang Goethe-Universitat, 6 volumes, 2nd edition, with an introduction by Fuat Sezgin.

Kane, Ousmane, "Shinqit," *Encyclopedia of Islam*, II.

Kane, Ousmane, " Sha'ir, West and Central Sudan," *Encyclopedia of Islam*, II.

Kane, Ousmane, "Sultan, West Africa", Encyclo *Encyclopedia of Islam*, II.

Kane, Ousmane, 1994, "Senegal," in G.J. Roper (ed.), *World Survey of Islamic Manuscripts*, Leiden E.J. Brill, volume 3, pp. 51-63.

Kane, Ousmane, 1997, *Handlist of Islamic Manuscripts, Senegal*, London, Al-Furqan.

Kane, Ousmane, 2003, *Muslim Modernity in Postcolonial Northern Nigeria: A study of the Society for the Removal of Innovation and Reinstatement of Tradition*, Leiden, E.J. Brill.

Kane, Ousmane and Hunwick, John, 2002a, Seeseman R.,"Tijani Writers of the Niassene Tradition", in Hunwick John (comp.) *Arabic Literature of Africa: The Writings of Western Sudanic Africa*, Leiden, E.J. Brill.

Kane, Ousmane and Hunwick, John, 2002b, "Other Tijani Writers of Senegambia", in Hunwick John (comp.) *Arabic Literature of Africa. The Writings of Western Sudanic Africa*, Leiden, E. J. Brill.

Kane, Ousmane and Hunwick, John, 2002c, "Murid Writers of Senegambia", in Hunwick John (comp.) *Arabic Literature of Africa. The Writings of Western Sudanic Africa*, Leiden, E. J. Brill.

Kane, Ousmane and Hunwick, John, 2002 (d), "Other Senegambian Writers", in Hunwick John (ed.) *Arabic Literature of Africa: The Writings of Western Sudanic Africa*, Leiden, E. J. Brill.

Kane, Ousmane and Triaud, Jean-Louis, *Islam et islamisme au sud du Sahara*, Paris, Karthala, 1998.

Kani, Ahmed, 1984, *The Intellectual Origin of the Sokoto Jihad*, Ibadan, Imam Publications.

Kepel, Gilles & Richard, Yann (eds.), 1990, *Intellectuels et militants de l'islam contemporain*, Paris, Seuil.

Kepel, Gilles, 2000, *Jihad, expansion et déclin de l'islamisme*, Paris, Gallimard.

Khader, Bichara, 1996, "L'islam et la modernité", in Girard Andrée (ed.) *Clefs pour l'Islam. Du religieux au politique. Des origines aux enjeux d'aujourd'hui*, Bruxelles, GRIP, pp. 147-153.

Knappert, Jan, "The Transmission of Knowledge: A Note on the Islamic Literatures of Africa", *Sudanic Africa*, 7, 1996, pp.169-164.

Knappert, Jan, 1988, "The Function of Arabic in the Islamic Ritual", *Journal for Islamic Studies*, 8 novembre, pp. 42-52.

Knappert, Jan, 1990, "The Islamic Poetry of Africa", *Journal of Islamic Studies*, pp. 91-140.

Koelle, Sigmund W., 1970, *African Native Literature: Proverbs, Tales, Fables and Historical Fragments in the Kanuri or Borno Language*, To which are added a Translation of the Above and a Kanuri English Vocabulary, Freeport, New York.

Kyari, Tijani, "The Shuwa Arabs", 1986, in Adamu, Mahdi & Kirk-Greene A., (eds.) *Pastoralists of the West African Savanna*, Manchester, Manchester University Press in association with the International African Institute.

Laïdi, Zaki (dir.), 1998, *Géopolitique du sens*, Paris, Desclée de Bouwer.

Lar, Mary, 1989, *Aspects of Nomadic Education in Nigeria*, Jos, Fab Education Books.

Last, Murray, "Reform in West Africa: Jihad Movements in the Nineteenth Century", in Ade Ajayi J. F. ; Crowder Michael, *History of West Africa*, London, Longman, 1985, vol 2, pp. 1-47.

Last, Murray, 1967, *The Sokoto Caliphate*, London, Longman.

Lema, A. A., 1976, "The Integration of Formal and Non-formal Education", *Education in East Africa Journal*, vol. 6, 2, pp. 99-111.

Leveau, Rémy, 1992, "Les mouvements islamiques", *Pouvoirs*, 62, 45-58.

Levtzion, Nehemia and Hopkins, J.F.P. (eds.) 1981, *Corpus of Early Arabic Sources for West African History*, Cambridge, London, New York, Melbourne, Sydney, Cambridge University Press.

Levtzion, Nehemia, 1971, "A Seventeenth Century Chronicle by Ibn Al-Mukhtar: A Critical Study of Tarikh al-Fattash", *BSOAS*, vol XXXIV, 3, pp. 571-593.

Levtzion, Nehemia, 1985, "The Early States of the Western Sudan", in Ade Ajayi J. F. and Crowder Michael, *History of West Africa*, London, Longman, vol. 1, 3rd edition, pp. 129-166.

Lewis, Bernard, 1988, *Le langage politique de l'islam*, Paris, Galllimard.

Lofchie, Michael, 1994, "The New Political Economy of Africa", in Apter David; Rosberg Carl, *Political Development and the New Realism in Sub-Saharan Africa*, Charlottesville and London, University Press of Virginia, pp. 145-183.

Loimeier, Roman, "Cheikh Touré: Du réformisme à l'islamisme, un musulman sénégalais dans le siècle", *Islam et sociétés au sud du Sahara*, 8, 1994, pp. 55-66.

Loimeier, Roman, 1997, *Islamic Reform and Political Change in Northern Nigeria*, Evanston, Northwestern University Press.

Lovejoy, Paul, 1978, "Notes on the *Asl al-Wangariyyin*", *Kano Studies*, (1), 3, pp. 46-52

Ly Madina, 1972, "Quelques remarques sur le Tarikh el-Fettash", *Bulletin de l'IFAN*, T.XXXIV, sér. B, n° 32, pp. 471-493.

Magassouba, Moriba,1985, *L'islam au Sénégal. Et demain les mollahs?*, Paris, Karthala.

Malamba, Gilombe Mudiji, 1989, *Le language des masques africains: Étude des formes et fonctions symboliques des "Mbuya" des Phende*, Kinshasa, Facultés catholiques de Kinshasa.

Martin, Jean-Yves, 1982, "Sociologie de l'enseignement en Afrique noire", in Santerre, R. & Mercier-Tremblay C. (eds.) *La Quête du savoir: Essais pour une anthropologie de l'éducation camerounaise*, Montréal, Les Presses de l'Université de Montréal, pp. 545-579.

Mattes, Hanspeter, 1993, "La daʿwa libyenne entre le coran et le livre vert", in Otayek René, *Le radicalisme islamique au sud du Sahara: Daʿwa, arabisation et critique de l'Occident*, Paris, Karthala, pp. 37-73.

Mazrui, Ali A., 1976, A *World Federation of Cultures: An African Perspective*, New York, The Free Press.

Mbaïosso, A., 1990, *L'éducation au Tchad: Bilan, problèmes et perspectives*, Paris, Karthala.

Mbacké, Khadim, 1996, *Les Bienfaits de l'éternel ou la biographie de Cheikh Ahmadu Bamba*, Dakar.

Mbaye, El-Hadji Ravane, 1976, "L'islam au Sénégal", PhD thesis in Islamic Studies, University of Dakar.

Mbaye, El-Hadji Ravane and Mbaye, Babacar, 1975, "Supplément au catalogue des manuscrits de l'IFAN", *Bulletin de l'Institut Fondamental d'Afrique Noire*, série B, 37, pp. 878-895.

Mercier-Tremblay, C., 1982, "[Savoir traditionnel] Présentation", in Santerre, R. & Mercier-Tremblay C. (eds.) *La Quête du savoir: Essais pour une anthropologie de l'éducation camerounaise*, Montréal, Les Presses de l'Université de Montréal, pp. 67-71.

Monteil, Vincent, 1965, "Les manuscrits historiques arabo-africains: Bilan provisoire", *Bulletin de l'Institut Fondamental d'Afrique Noire,* B, 27, pp. 531-542.

Monteil, Vincent, 1966, "Les manuscrits historiques arabo-africains. Bilan provisoire", *Bulletin de l'Institut Fondamental d'Afrique Noire,* B, 28, pp. 668-675.

Mudimbe, V., 1988, *The Invention of Africa: Gnosis, Philosophy and the Order of Knowledge*, Bloomington and Indianapolis, Indiana University Press.

Mudimbe, V., 1991, *Parables and Fables: Exegesis, Textuality and Politics in Central Africa*, Madison, The University of Wisconsin, Press.

Mudimbe, V., 1994, *The Idea of Africa*, Bloomington, Indianapolis, London, Indiana University Press & James Currey.

Mugo, M., 1987 "Culture and Imperialism" communication paper presented at the International Conference "Intellectuals, the State and Imperialism", Harare, University of Zimbabwe, 20-22 October.

Muhammad, Baba Yunus (comp.) and Hunwick, John (ed.), 1995, *Handlist of Islamic Manuscripts*. National Archives, Kaduna, London, Al-Furqan, vol. 1.

Muhammad, Baba Yunus (comp.) and Hunwick, John (ed.), 1997, *Handlist of Islamic Manuscripts,* National Archives, Kaduna, London, Al-Furqan, vol. 2.

Muhammad, Baba Yunus (comp.) and Hunwick, John (ed.), 2001, *Handlist of Islamic Manuscripts, Nigeria,* The University of Ibadan Library, London, Al-Furqan.

Nahwi, al-Khalil, *Bilad al-Shinqit*, al-manara wa al-ribat, Tunis, ISESCO.

Nda, Paul, 1987, *Les intellectuels et le pouvoir en Afrique noire*, Paris, L'Harmattan.

Nda, Paul, 1987, *Pouvoir, lutte de classes, idéologie et milieu intellectuel africain*, Paris, Présence africaine.

Ndayako, Samuila, 1972, *The Problems of Education in Northern States of Nigeria*, Kaduna, Baraka Press.

Neogy, Rajat, 1987, "On Being an African Intellectual", paper delivered at the International Conference "Intellectuals, *The State and Imperialism*, Harare, University of Zimbabwe, 20-22 October.

Normann, Hans; Snyman, Ina and Cohen, Morris, 1996, *Indigenous Knowledge and its Use in Southern Africa*, Pretoria, Human Science Research Council.

Nyang, Suleiman, 1982, "Saudi Arabian Foreign Policy toward Africa", *Horn of Africa* 5, 2, pp. 3-17.

O'Fahey, Sean, 1994, *Arabic Literature of Africa. I. The Writings of Eastern Sudanic Africa to c. 1900,* Leiden, E. J. Brill.

Otayek, René (ed), 1993, *Le radicalisme islamique au sud du Sahara: Da'wa, arabisation et critique de l'Occident*, Paris, Karthala.

Ouane, A. (ed.), 1996, *Vers une culture multilingue de l'éducation*, Paris, L'Harmattan.

Ould Cheikh, Abdel Wedoud, 1987, "[Compte rendu de] Rohkatalog der arabischen handschriften in Mauretanien", *Islam et sociétés au sud du Sahara*, 1, pp.109-113.

Ould Cheikh, Abdel Wedoud,1988, *Eléments d'histoire de la Mauritanie*, Nouakchott, Centre culturel français.

Ould Eli, Sidi Amar (comp.) and Johansen, Julian (ed.), 1995, *Handlist of Manuscripts in the Centre de Documentation et de Recherches Historiques Ahmad Baba Timbuctu*, London, Al-Furqan, vol. 1, mss 1 to 1500.

Paden, John Naber, 1986, *Ahmadu Bello, Sardauna of Sokoto: Values and leadership in Nigeria*, Zaria, Hudahuda Publishing Company.

Pondopoulo, Anna, "Une traduction 'mal partie' 1923-1945 : Le *Zuhur al-basatin* de Cheikh Mussa Kamara", *Islam et sociétés au sud du Sahara*, 7, 1993, pp. 95-110.

Pontie, Danielle and Pontie Guy, 1982, "Organisation sociale et éducation traditionnelle chez les Guiziga", in Santerre, R. & Mercier-Tremblay C. (dirs.), *La Quête du savoir. Essais pour une anthropologie de l'éducation camerounaise*, Montréal, Les Presses de l'université de Montréal, 104-121.

Prunier, Gérard, "Le mouvement des ansars au Soudan depuis la fin de l'Etat mahdiste", in Kane Ousmane; Triaud Jean-Louis, *Islam et islamisme au sud du Sahara*, Paris, Karthala, 1998, pp. 41-58.

Rahman, Fazlur, 1970, "Revival and Reform in Islam", *Cambridge History of Islam*, vol. 2 b, pp. 632-656.

Rebstock, Ulrich, 1985, *Rohkatalog Der Arabischen Handschriften in Mauretanien*, Tubingen.

Robinson, David, 1988, *La guerre sainte d'al-Hajj Umar: Le Soudan occidental au milieu du XIXe siècle*, Paris, Karthala.

Robinson, David ; Triaud Jean-Louis (eds.), 1997, *Le temps des marabouts. Itinéraires et stratégies islamiques en Afrique occidentale française v. 1880-1960*, Paris, Karthala.

Roper, G. J. (ed.), 1994, *World Survey of Islamic Manuscripts,* Leiden, E.J. Brill, 4 vols.

Saad, N. Elias, 1983, *Social History of Timbuctu: The Role of Muslim Scholars and Notables 1400-1900*, Cambridge, Cambridge University Press.

Samb, Amar, 1973, *Matraqué par le destin ou la vie d'un talibé*, Dakar et Abdjan, Les Nouvelles éditions africaines.

Samb, Amar, 1972, *Contribution du Sénégal à la littérature d'expression arabe*, Dakar, IFAN.

Sanneh, Lamin, 1979, *The Jakhanke. The History of an Islamic Clerical People of the Senegambia*, London, International African Institute.

Santerre, R. & Mercier-Tremblay C. (eds.), 1982, *La Quête du savoir: Essais pour une anthropologie de l'éducation camerounaise*, Montréal, Les Presses de l'Université de Montréal.

Santerre, R., "Maîtres coraniques de Maroua", in Santerre R. & Mercier-Tremblay C. (eds.), *La Quête du savoir: Essais pour une anthropologie de l'éducation camerounaise*, Montréal, Les Presses de l'université de Montréal, 1982, pp. 350-371.

Santerre, R., 1973, *Pédagogie musulmane d'Afrique noire: L'école coranique peule au Cameroun*, Montréal, Les Presses de l'Université de Montréal.

Santerre, R., 1982, "Aspects conflictuels de deux systèmes d'enseignement au Nord-Cameroun", in Santerre R. & Mercier-Tremblay C. (eds.), *La Quête du savoir: Essais pour une anthropologie de l'éducation camerounaise*, Montréal, Les Presses de l'Université de Montréal, pp. 396-413.

Santerre, R., 1982, "La pédagogie coranique", in Santerre R. & Mercier-Tremblay C. (eds.), *La Quête du savoir: Essais pour une anthropologie de l'éducation camerounaise*, Montréal, Les Presses de l'Université de Montréal, pp. 337-349.

Santerre, R., 1982, "Africanisme et science de l'éducation", in Santerre R. & Mercier-Tremblay C. (eds.), *La Quête du savoir: Essais pour une anthropologie de l'éducation camerounaise*, Montréal, Les Presses de l'Université de Montréal, pp. 30-46.

Santerre, R., 1982, "L'éducation camerounaise", in Santerre R. & Mercier-Tremblay C. (eds.), *La Quête du savoir: Essais pour une anthropologie de l'éducation camerounaise*, Montréal, Les Presses de l'Université de Montréal, pp. 23-29.

Santerre, R., 1982, "Linguistique et politique au Cameroun", in Santerre R. & Mercier-Tremblay C. (eds.), *La Quête du savoir: Essais pour une anthropologie de l'éducation camerounaise*, Montréal, Les Presses de l'université de Montréal, pp. 47-57.

Schmitz, J., (ed.), 1998, *Florilège au jardin de l'Histoire des Noirs: L'aristocratie peule et la révolution islamique des clercs musulmans (Vallée du Fleuve Sénégal)*, Paris, Editions du CNRS.

Seydou, Christiane, 1986, "Aspects de la littérature peul", in Adamu, Mahdi; Kirk-Greene A. (eds.) *Pastoralists of the West African Savanna*, Manchester, Manchester University Press in association with the International African Institute.

Sifawa, Abdullahi Muhammad, 1988, *Research in Islam: A Catalogue of Dissertations on Islam in Nigeria, Sokoto*, Centre for Islamic Studies, University of Sokoto.

Stewart, Charles, Ahmed Salim Ould Sidi Ahmad and Ould Ahmad Muhammad Yahya, 1990, "Catalogue of Arabic Manuscripts at the Institut mauritanien de recherche scientifique", *Islam et sociétés au sud du Sahara*, 4, pp. 179-184.

Sukhraj, Penny, "Mbecki Appeals to SA Muslims to Save Historical Artefacts", *Sunday's Paper*, March 31 2002 p.1

Touré, Hasseye Abdourahamane, "Les universités tombouctiennes : grandeur et décadence", *Mots pluriels*, 12, déc. 99, http://www.arts.uwa.edu.au/Mots Pluriels/MP1299aht.html.

Tourneux, Henry and Iyebi-Mandjek Olivier, 1994, *L'école dans une petite ville africaine* (Maroua, Cameroun), Paris, Karthala.

Triaud, Jean-Louis, 1998, "Introduction" in Kane Ousmane & Triaud Jean-Louis (eds.), *Islam et islamisme au sud du Sahara*, Paris, Karthala, pp. 7-20.

Triaud, Jean-Louis and Robinson, David (eds.) *La Tijaniyya: Une confrérie musulmane à la conquête de l'Afrique*, Paris, Karthala, 2000.

Triaud, Jean-Louis, 1988, "L'Université islamique du Niger", *Islam et sociétés au sud du Sahara*, 2, pp. 157-165.

Tsiga, Ismaila and Uba, Adamu Abdallah, (dirs.), 1997, *Islam and the History of Learning in Katsina*, Ibadan, Benin City, Kaduna, Lagos, Owerri, Spectrum Books Limited.

Uba Adamu, Abdalla, "Ajamization of Knowledge: Challenges and Prospects", unpublished paper.

Useen, Andrea, 1999, "Muslims in East Africa Develop their Own Higher Education Options", *Chronicle of Higher Education in Africa*, 13 novembre.

Van Beek, Wouter, 1982, "Les savoirs kapsiki", in Santerre R. & Mercier-Tremblay C. (eds.) *La Quête du savoir: Essais pour une anthropologie de l'éducation camerounaise*, Montréal, Les Presses de l'Université de Montréal, pp. 180-207.

Warren, Michael, Egunjobi Layi and Bolanle, Wahhab, 1996, *Indigenous Knowledge In Education*, Ibadan, Ageless Friendship Press, Ltd.

Wickramansinghe, Nira, 2001, "A Comment on African Modes of Self-Writing", *Identity, Culture and Politics: An Afro-Asian Dialogue*, (2) pp. 37-41.

Widding-Jacobson, A. and Westerlund, D., 1989, *Culture, Experience and Pluralism: Essays on African Ideas of Illness and Healing*, Uppsala, Centraltryckeriet A. B.